a Leisurely Ride Across France
by Alan P Kretchmar

Cover Photograph: Chateau d'Azay-le-Rideou

Author can be reached at: Kretchmar5@aol.com

Copyright © 2012

All rights reserved.

ISBN: 1470006162

ISBN 13: 9781470006167

Library of Congress Control Number: 2012902221
CreateSpace, North Charleston, SC

Table of Contents

D. LEG FOUR: BORDEAUX TO SPAIN — 129

"To Karen, my partner across France and through life."

Introduction

I guess I have always enjoyed bicycling. As a kid our bikes gave us the freedom to go to the beach or the mall on our own by the age of nine or ten. I first bicycled in Europe in 1971 when I bought a bike in Amsterdam at the Rembrandtsplein flea market and rode to Germany. My wife and I bicycled on our second date and later on we traveled through Maine by bicycle. In 1980 I convinced her to leave our four month old daughter and go back to Holland and bicycle as I did nine years earlier. We had a fantastic time riding from Amsterdam to Bruges, Belgium.. It was then that we decided to come back someday and continue the trip south and ride across France. It was a dream we kept on the backburner for over 20 years.

Fast forward to 2001. My daughter was living in Europe for the spring semester of her junior year in college. We made plans to visit her and at that point we realized the time had come to act on our dream. We made plans to return to Bruges and continue where we left off 21 years earlier. Our goal was to bicycle across France. We felt we could do it in four legs, riding about

200 miles per trip. It was to be our adventure for the next six years.

I think it's important for people to have a challenging distraction to work for. We get so caught up in our everyday life that something totally different from our everyday routine is mentally refreshing. I call this a QUASI-ADVENTURE since it is not really dangerous but it is certainly adventurous traveling alone across a foreign country. We were in our fifties when we began our quest and we knew we had to stay physically fit if we were to do this. We had to learn about the geography we would be entering and we had to figure out how to get bicycles and make travel arrangements. I can't say making arrangements were as much fun as the trip itself but it certainly was exciting putting the pieces of the travel puzzle together. We decided not to make too many reservations ahead of time. We also didn't want to use the internet. We wanted the excitement of riding into a town and finding hotels or B&Bs as we arrived. I didn't want to spend any travel time looking at a website.

But none of that can compare with getting on the bicycles after a year or two of planning and waiting. You glide away from your hotel at the start of your trip not knowing what experiences await you. You have such a feeling of freedom at that point. It is just two people on their bikes carrying all their belongings for the next week You just ride along not knowing what the day will hold in store for you, not knowing where or what you will eat or where you will spend the night. You don't know what castles or cathedrals you will be seeing that day or what markets or festivals you will happen upon. It's like being nine years old again and heading out on your own.

Leg One:
Bruges To Giverny

April, 2001

OUR ROUTE ACROSS FRANCE

BRUGES, BELGIUM

We arrived in Bruges on the Thalys high speed train from Paris at twilight. Carrying our backpacks, we crossed the large square outside the terminal and crossed the busy Koenig Albertlaan road and entered medieval Bruges.

Bruges is a beautiful city frozen in time. It's medieval buildings are crisscrossed by canals with graceful stone bridges. In the 13th century Bruges was one of the wealthiest cities in Europe. Its wealth was from textiles. Wool was imported from England and woven into the finest cloth available by the 4000 weavers in Bruges. As we walked to our hotel the drizzle and evening light made the ancient buildings look mysterious.

We came to the Minnewater, a rectangular, broad lake that once thrived with merchant ships. This night the only activity on the lake were the swans gliding across the calm water. Across the lake the light of the Mill restaurant reflected on the water. Our hotel, the Hotel Egmond, was just beyond the restaurant. As we walked along we passed through the Begijnhof, a peaceful enclave founded to shelter the wives of the crusaders in 1244. It is now cobbled walkways surrounded by white gabled buildings and large shade trees. On the far side of the Minnewater we reached Hotel Egmond.

Hotel Egmond is located down a lane at the edge of a park. It is an old 18th century manor with a yellow brick exterior. There is a red tiled roof behind the stairstep gables of the main façade. The interior is complete with old wooden beamed ceilings, ornate fireplaces and the traditional black and white tile floors so common in Flemish paintings. Our room opened to the outside and faced the parklands.

We were met by Mrs. Van Laere, a woman in her early fifties. We sat in one of the comfortable sitting rooms off the lobby and had tea and cookies shaped like cigars called pirouettes. She was very calm when I told her my wallet was stolen on the Metro in Paris that morning and we had no cash, checks or credit cards! That morning I was victimized by a pickpocket while getting on the Metro in Paris. It was a classic mistake of rushing to get on a train as the doors were closing. As we squeezed on at the last minute a group of young men pointed to the cuffs of my pants and started cutting them. While my attention was on my shoe tops they lifted my wallet out of my back pocket. I realized what happened soon enough to curse them as they jumped off the train. We tried to file a report at the police station near Les Halles but because of communication difficulties and red tape we gave up. Maybe the gendarmes felt it was too trivial to bother with. We still had our train tickets so we decided to use them and correct the financial problem after we got to Bruges.

Mrs. Van Laere took our crisis in stride. She was kind enough to advance us 2200 Belgian francs or about $50. With the help of her son, I was able to get on the phone to American Express and get my travelers checks replaced and cancel my credit and ATM cards. They also gave us directions to the bicycle shops in Bruges along with their recommendations for the best shops to purchase our transportation to France. We did all we could do that evening to rectify our situation.

Leaving Hotel Egmond

Our room at Hotel Egmond opened to the outside parkland. It had a high ceiling of about ten or twelve feet. The floor was covered with cold tile but ample throw rugs warmed the room. The lower portion of the windows were hung with the traditional Belgian lace curtains and above the windows were uncovered. Our tasks for the next day were clear. Get money and get our bicycles.

GETTING CASH
AND BICYCLES

I decided to get up early and take the train to Ghent to get our travelers checks replaced. I found out that the American Express office in Bruges requires a police report to refund the checks but surprisingly the Ghent office didn't. Since we didn't file a report at the Parisian police station, I felt I needed to go to Ghent.

Getting to Ghent was easy enough. Finding the office was not. A quick thirty minute train ride covered the twenty miles to Ghent and let me off in the central station. I got directions to the office and jumped on a trolley-type vehicle and rode about ten minutes to my stop. Easy enough. I walked down the street looking for number 356. On arriving I found there was no American Express office at that address. I walked up and down the block without any luck. I went into a travel agency across the street from number 356. They told me that the office was no longer there and the owner was a crook. Great! What now? Catty-corner was an office that looked like a financial business. Perhaps they could help me. I got in a line and after a ten minute wait I got to the clerk. She spoke very good English and informed me that I was at the American Express office. I looked around the rooms and couldn't understand why there were to signs or logos in view. In a few minutes she replaced my travelers checks. I retraced my path and was back in Bruges by noon.

That afternoon we set out to find bicycles. With map in hand we found our first shop at the end of one of the cities traditional cobblestone streets. There were a couple of used mountain bikes that didn't look comfortable for riding and didn't look like they would hold up long enough to get us out of the city. We walked through the medieval streets to our next shop that sold bicycles and motorcycles. They had nothing but super expensive competition bikes. Finally at Halford's, a rather modern shop just down the street from the large medieval market square, we found new bikes with six gears, luggage racks and kick stands. I asked the clerk the cost for the Eurostyle brand bikes. "Twelve hundred Belgian francs," he informed us. That was about $175 a piece. "We'll take these two." The clerk said it will take about half an hour to get the bicycles ready so we went for a late lunch across the street at a restaurant called Peter Pancake. It was already 3:30 so we were famished. The pancakes were crepes with egg and ham rolled inside and were very satisfying. We finished with a traditional Belgian waffle generously sprinkled with sugar.

After our lunch we went back to pick up our bikes. The clerk said they were all ready to go. When we went to pay for them we were told they wouldn't accept the traveler's checks I had just gotten in Ghent. Of course our credit and ATM cards were somewhere in Paris. He told us there was a bank around the corner that will cash our checks. So off we went to the bank. I pushed on the door and it didn't budge. It was locked. I looked through the window at the teller. She pointed at her watch. They closed at 4:00 P.M. on Fridays. It was now 4:10. Back we went to Halford's. They said they were open to 7:00 P.M. that evening if we could cash our checks. We walked back to Hotel Egmond. The city was starting to empty out. The tourists were walking away from the city center and the traffic was heavy as people were leaving for the weekend. At the hotel I explained to Mme. Van Leare that I needed cash to buy the bikes. Together with her husband they started going through the days receipts. He went through his pockets and her purse. They were able to muster enough cash for our bicycles. "Thank you so much. I think we will be able to get started tomorrow as we originally planned despite our unfortunate events." We headed back to the bike shop where our brand new Eurostyle bikes were waiting for us. We settled our bill and rode back to the hotel on the bumpy, cobblestone streets. As we rode back the evening light gave the medieval buildings and canals of Bruges a mysterious appearance.

Having our hotel room open to the outside made it very easy to wheel our bikes right into our room. After dinner we packed our bags and panniers to make sure the bike racks would hold all our belongings. Things seemed to fit on well. That night while trying to sleep a heavy hail storm rolled through. We laid in bed listening to the hailstones pelt the windows and the wind whistle through the cracks around the door. What will the weather be tomorrow? Will we have to start in a storm? The morning will tell. We had a difficult time falling back asleep wondering what it will be like when we start the journey we waited twenty years for.

ON TO FRANCE

The next morning we awoke to a bright, sunny albeit cold day. Temperatures were in the low 40's. We dressed warmly and went for breakfast in the dining room decorated with its dark oak paneling and heavy ceiling beams. There was a warm fire in the stone fireplace. We ate a breakfast of cold meats and cheeses with fresh breads and rolls. We finished with koeken, a sweet, buttery pastry topped with various spices, nuts or raisins. There was always ample strong coffee.

We rode our newly acquired bicycles into the center of Bruges. I had to pick up extra cash that was wired to me. At 9:00AM I was the first to queue up at the American Express office and was able to get it without any difficulty. I asked if I could get travelers checks or French francs but all they could dispense was Belgian francs. This would have repercussions for the next several days.

The old medieval center of Bruges was brimming with people that morning. I'm sure they were exclusively tourists. We stopped at a weekly flea market. We were tempted by old brass mirrors and wooden cookie molds but soon came to the realization that we couldn't carry any extra items, at least this early in our ride. We looked at tapestries in some of the local shops. Karen broke down and bought a zippered purse covered with a tapestry displaying peasants at work in the fields. It would fit into our bags without taking up much room. We finally rode back to Hotel Egmond. We packed our panniers and backpacks on the bikes. We put on all the layers of clothing we had to wear. It was still frosty outside but a bright sun made it feel better. We said adieu to Mme. Van Laere and at about 11AM we were finally ready to continue our journey that began twenty-one years ago in Amsterdam.

We left Bruges heading south on the N64 road. The terrain was flat and to our surprise there were bike paths bordering the roads. We made good time cruising through Torhout and Kortemark. We rode the very quiet N70 into Ypres. The land was mostly farmland. The cemeteries were ubiquitous in this area of Flanders. Most of what we saw were British, Australian and New Zealand graves with their white headstones arranged in orderly rows. Late in the afternoon, in the town of Messen, we road down a short dead-end street and got our first view of France in the distance. As we rode further, I realized there was no designation for the border and the N69 road continued into France. I had no idea when we actually crossed into France. There was no checkpoint and no signs. I expected to see a large welcome sign somewhere but the only way we knew we were in France was the language on the shops and signs changed from Dutch to French. We knew we had arrived in France.

We reached the city of Armentieres, made famous by it's mademoiselle in the World War I song, around 5 PM. It was only ten or fifteen miles south of the border. We were actually feeling quite energetic after our afternoon ride. We rode down the main street past the massive city hall. I assumed we'd find a hotel right near there but it took us a good forty-five minutes to find one. We finally stayed at the Hotel Joly. It had a sedate looking edifice. Our room had sheets and curtains with bright blue seashell patterns. I felt like we were having an overnight slumber party. It was quite comfortable and our first day of biking was not too physically demanding. We had dinner right across the street in a pub named the Buffoon that had a cheerful atmosphere. It seemed like there were many families dining together. We had a nice dinner of crepes on the second floor landing overlooking the diners below. When it came time to pay Belgian francs were gladly accepted for payment. We walked back across the street to Hotel Joly and had no trouble falling asleep that night under our seashell bedspread.

A DAY WITHOUT MEALS

The next morning was again bright and clear. We had breakfast in the enormous dining room which would have been more appropriate for a banquet than two travelers eating breakfast. Evidently the Hotel Joly dining room can be used for private parties but this morning we were the only people present. The room had massive oak mantled fireplaces and intricately carved wood paneling covering the walls up to the ten foot ceiling. On finishing breakfast we were able to pay our bill in Belgian francs again and we set out from the courtyard on our bikes through the busy streets of Armentieres.

The land to the south was more hilly and there were no longer bike paths. We rode out of Armentieres on D171 to Nueve-Chapelle. The road was very quiet without much traffic. We encountered many, perhaps hundreds, of cyclists in their colorful logo filled shirts reminiscent of the "Tour de France." We never knew if we were among a competition or just seeing Frenchmen enjoying a Sunday morning ride. The land here was rolling farmland with occasional forests. About one o'clock we entered the town of Noeux-les-Mines. In the center of this pleasant town across from the turnabout we saw a café with big picture windows overlooking their patio. It looked like a good spot for us to stop for lunch. We locked up our bikes and went in. After looking over the menu and realizing how hungry we were, we ordered bowls of warm onion soup and crepes. I did remember to ask our waitress if they accepted Belgian francs. "No" was the emphatic answer to that question. The answer was also no to American dollars. The answer was also no to travelers checks. Only French francs were accepted. Evidently we were too far from the border with Belgium to use our money. Disappointed, we left the café. "We'll find another restaurant where they'll accept our Belgian money." At the next three places we stopped the answer was always the same. We soon realized we were not going to have lunch that day. With the last 15 or 20 French francs we had left from Paris we went into a tabac, a small convenience shop, and bought a box of cookies and oranges. We lunched in the luxury of a bench in a bus stop shelter. So much for a leisurely lunch in the French countryside.

We decided not to ride too late in the day since we had trouble finding a hotel even in a large town like Armentieres. There certainly were no towns near that size on our itinerary that evening. We decided to stop around 5 P.M. and look for our nights lodging. In the morning we would go to a bank and exchange our Belgian money and cash the travelers checks to pay the lodging bill. We thought Avesnes-le-Comte looked like a good destination. We rode straight south along D75 through Cambligneul and Aubigny-en-Artois on our way to Avesnes. As we rode into the medium sized town we approached a couple walking down the street and asked directions to a hotel. After careful thought they said there might be one next to the marie or city hall. We thanked them and took off in that direction. After going up and down the street a few times without seeing a hotel we saw the same couple catch up to us. We told them we couldn't find the hotel. They waved down a car of gendarmes who concurred that there was no hotel in Avesnes-le-Comte. But they did inform us of a bed and breakfast in the town of Hauteville. This was about six kilometers away. Having little choice in the matter, we rode toward Hauteville in the early evening. It was seemingly was a total uphill ride to the town. On reaching the town we found the suggested Bed and Breakfast. We knocked on the door and no one answered. It seemed there was no one there. As we were leaving we saw an elderly woman walking across the street with her grandchildren. We asked her if she knew if the B&B was open. She was not able to understand us but she motioned for us to follow her and led us to her home down the road. We followed her down the gravel driveway and went into her small ranch-style house. Inside her son made a phone call to the B&B and confirmed that it was closed. After a few more calls he found a room in a B&B in Fossieux. Unfortunately, Fossieux was the next town to the south and another five kilometers away. He said he would lead us out of Hauteville and onto the correct road. He jumped on his bike and we followed him to the edge of town. There he brought us to the road leading to Fosseux and motioned for us to continue that way. We bid him adieu as we headed south in the diminishing, evening light.

It was now 7:30 and turning into twilight as we climbed the hill up to Fosseux. We rode past an 18th chateau that probably controlled the town's population of about two hundred people. We circled around to the ancient church and found our B&B at the edge of the churchyard. It was a white house surrounded by flowers with "1849" over the door. Mrs. Bouchard welcomed us in with coffee and cookies. After not having dinner, the snacks were extremely appreciated. We looked forward to a restful night after almost eight hours of bicycling. Mrs. Bouchard offered to drive us to the next town where there was a restaurant. I knew we didn't have the means to pay for dinner so I just asked her to drive us the next morning to cash our Belgian money and travelers checks. She said it is Monday and the banks are closed in this area. Evidently banking hours vary from area to area and here they were closed on Monday. I didn't say anything else because I didn't want to leave the B&B. So we ate the rest of our cookies and oranges and waited for breakfast. As we turned in early I tried to figure out how we were going to pay tomorrow.

INTO AMIENS

The next morning we awoke after a restful night. We asked to eat breakfast at 7 A.M. so we could get an early start. The breakfast of eggs, cereal, toast and fruit was our first meal in about 24 hours so we really devoured everything we could get our hands on. I explained to Madam Bouchard that we had no cash or credit cards but my traveler's checks would be acceptable as payment for the room. She agreed to accept them. Then I had to explain the value of the checks were more than the cost of the room charge and she actually owed us some francs back in change. This was accomplished even though she spoke no English. She evidently trusted us and we received francs from her in change. I'm sure she was relieved when she cashed the traveler's checks when the banks finally opened on Tuesday.

We again resolved not to ride too late today since we really finished in the early evening hours on our first two days of riding. Our goal of Amiens was only about 30 miles away and we wanted to stop in the early afternoon and act like normal tourists and enjoy the cathedral city's sights. By about 9 A.M. we said adieu to Madam Bouchard and her lovely cottage and glided past the old church and headed south along the country roads. Again we were fortunate to have sunny and cool weather during our morning ride.

The ride was relatively easy that morning. We rode in rolling hills and farmlands and through small villages like Sombrin and Couturelle to the west. At Pas-en-Artois we got on highway D11 and had straight shot southwest to Amiens. We didn't stop to eat lunch even though we had cash to spend. We remained satiated after our large breakfast in Fosseux. We arrived around 2 P.M. and started negotiating traffic in the large city of 120,000. As we approached the city's center on the Somme river, we could see the Amiens Cathedral dominating the skyline on the opposite bank of the river.

Amiens Cathedral from the Somme River

We decided to quickly get a hotel and not waste time searching. We headed straight to the Hotel de Normandie mentioned in our guide book. The hotel was slightly crusty but the location and price were agreeable. Plus it had a garage where we could store our bikes. We checked in quickly and ventured out on foot to explore the city.

We headed toward the cathedral on one of the pedestrian streets. We soon found out that banks in Amiens were open on Mondays. At the first bank we came to we cashed our traveler's checks and remaining Belgian francs. We felt like we were delivered from poverty and now had plenty of cash to eat or shop or whatever. It had been a little unnerving to travel with no money. Next stop was one of the little sidewalk creperies for some lunch. We ordered two crepes and an apple desert crepe inside the shop and went out to sit at one of the tables on the street. It was relaxing to sit down and eat although it was overcast and cool at this time in the afternoon.

We walked a few more blocks to the Notre-Dame Cathedral of Amiens. Work began on the largest cathedral in France in 1220. The wealth to construct it came from the cultivation of the plant woad, used to produce a blue dye. It was built to house the head of John the Baptist brought back from the Crusades to Amiens in1206. On completion it was twice the size of Notre Dame in Paris. We toured the magnificent nave and marveled at the wooden carved choir stalls and the hundreds of carved stone figures on the screens around the chancel and on the west porch.

On leaving the cathedral we crossed the Somme river, which was close to flood stage, and toured St. Leu, an area of artisans' shops and restaurants along the river. We wandered further to the Les Hortillonages, an area of water gardens among currently flooding canals. It was too muddy to venture off the paved sidewalks into the gardens. As we returned it began to rain, something the city along the river Somme didn't need. We still had a delightful dinner at Le Capitan at the rivers edge. The carbonnade beef stew was my first sit down dinner in almost two days. We ate at an outdoor table enclosed by temporary plastic sheets with space heaters. We could peer out from our table and see the magnificent cathedral across the river through the drizzly night.

FRENCH HOSPITALITY

The next morning we rode out of the dry garage at the Hotel de Normandie into a cool, rainy morning. It was delightful to ride down the pedestrian street Rue Lamartine in the town center. Before we ventured too far we stopped for a French breakfast. Along with our coffees, I had a chocolate brioche. Karen always wanted cereal and eggs but that was very hard to find. She had to settle for a nice buttery croissant.

It's not too difficult to find your way into the center of a city but finding your way out is another story. While trying to find a suitable bike route out of Amiens going south we stopped at an intersection and pondered our poorly detailed city map. An elderly man in his lorry approached us. He asked us if we needed directions and if we were English. In our best French we told him we were Americans and we did need directions. We told him we were heading south in the direction of Conty. He motioned for us to follow him and he took off in his truck. It was very hard for us to keep up with him as he weaved up and down tiny side streets. He finally stopped and got out. He said he used to drive a lorry delivering in central Europe but had to retire since he had heart surgery. He was kind enough to show us the surgical scars on his chest. I guess he was just a friendly old guy with time on his hands. He pointed out the road to Conty and we thanked him and pedaled off.

The road to Conty, highway D8, went through a green, forested valley and although it was a rainy morning it was a pleasant ride. In Conty we stopped for a snack at a country inn set back off the road. Since it was still too early for lunch we had coffee and a piece of apple pie. Anything out of the rain and warm felt good at that moment. We left the café in a slow drizzle and followed the Selle river south through farmland and heavily wooded patches.

We arrived in Crevecoeur-le-Grande around one o'clock. After riding through the town once and not seeing a café, we returned to the town center. We asked a man leaving a doctor's office where we could eat. He told us there was a pizza parlor around the corner. I asked him if he was the doctor and although he spoke no English he conveyed that he was. I explained I also am a doctor in the United States and work in a town named Creve Coeur. We said adieu and rode over to the restaurant. We were locking our bikes when he appeared again and motioned for us to follow him. I thought he was leading us to another restaurant and we followed him a few blocks and soon left the business area. In another block we arrived at a residence. He had brought us to his home. It was a nice two-story home on a residential street. He introduced us to his wife Cecile. Fortuitously, she taught English in the local high school so we were able to converse with her. Her two teenage boys were home since this was their spring break. We were invited to stay for lunch. We were still rather damp and Karen asked to use the bathroom before we ate. Cecile got Karen a set of towels and took her to the bathroom with a shower. I guess our communications weren't as good as we thought because Cecile thought Karen asked to take a shower. We told her that was unnecessary.

After shedding our wet outer clothes we sat in the kitchen for lunch. We did use their clothes drier while we ate. Cecile first brought out a serving bowl of sliced fresh cucumbers. I whispered to Karen I hope this isn't the whole meal because I'm really hungry. After that she brought out bowls of a thick lentil soup which were very filling. At this point I was well nourished but she immediately brought a platter of meats including my first taste of andouille sausage containing tripe and chitterlings. There was also a never ending supply of French bread. Next she brought out fresh strawberries and ice cream. We were satiated by this point but we were then lead into the living room for coffee and chocolates.

After a nice hour and a half unhurried visit we took photos of our French hosts in their front yard. We were again ready to continue on our journey. They told us we could find lodgings for the night in the ancient town of Gerberoy about fifteen miles away. We said adieu to Dr. Lestienne and his family and were again on our way to the southwest. Outside of Crevecoeur-le-Grand we cycled on a narrow road on a very flat plateau with extremely gusty headwinds. At times it seem like we weren't even moving and if a large truck sped past us in the opposite direction we actually were blown to a stop. We could look down from our plateau and see quaint villages like Marseille-en-Beauvasis and Songeons from above. After battling the wind we arrived at Gerberoy on a late, cloudy afternnon

Gerberoy was an English garrison town built during the Hundred Years War to house the English families staying there. We had to walk our bikes up a long, cobblestone road at the entrance to the village. We looked for the hotels or B&B's that were supposed to be there. As we entered the hill town we saw a hotel/restaurant with it lights on. As I walked up to the door the lights went out. The door was locked and no one responded to my knocking. I guess we weren't wanted there. We rode farther into the town as the sky darkened. We saw no one outside. The two-storied contiguous buildings looked like a facade from a movie set. We saw no place to stay as well as no people to ask. Finally, we saw three very nicely dressed people walking toward us. They seemed ghostly walking toward us in the drizzly light. One was on elderly woman in her 70's wearing a Burberry plaid cape and matching skirt who spoke fairly good English. The others were a stylishly dressed couple in their late 30's. It was strange to see people dressed like they should be dining in Paris in an isloated setting like this. She explained that many people have purchased these ancient houses for weekend retreats in the country. She also confirmed that there was no lodgings in Gerberoy. She suggested we walk down to Mister Tom's house. They took us down the street. Tom was an Englishman refinishing one of the elegant houses. His front parlor was an exquisite library with marble statues on pedestals and portraits of English gentlemen on the walls. He told us he stayed at a bed and breakfast while his house was uninhabitable. The inn was ran by Madame Simone who was the best cook in the area. We would not want to miss her dinners. Besides, he added, there is no other place to stay. He called over to the B&B and made us a reservation and then drew us a rather confusing map to the inn. We thanked him and parted company with our stylish acquaintances. We walked back to our bikes and realized we had another hour ride ahead of us. The light rain we were walking in quickly turned into a downpour. At the end of the row of houses was an open meeting area with several benches and tables under a gabled roof. We brought our bicycles into the protected area and decided to wait out the rain. It was cozy sitting there looking out at the ancient houses through the misty late afternoon. We snacked from our supply of cookies. At times there seemed to be people looking out of their houses through their curtains at us and wondering who were these people were sitting in the rain.

Waiting for the rain to let up in Giberoy

When it looked like the rain wasn't going to stop we decided we had better go on before we lost the daylight. We put on all of our raingear, which made us water-repellant but not water resistant, and started out into the rainy evening. Gerberoy left an eerie impression on us as we looked back as we rode down the hill into the countryside again.

Madam Simone's inn was in the town of St.Quentin-de-Pres. There were two ways to get there. One was on the busy road. It was longer and on a rainy night much more dangerous. The other took us through a maze of farming roads through small villages where each town was named H-court, like Hecourt and Haincourt and Hevecourt. We decided to take the later route. The roads were not well marked and unpaved. There was no traffic and it was actually a beautiful rural area with misty views. At times the rain lightened up enough for us to enjoy the scenery. Dripping wet we got from Bellefontaine to Haincourt to Hecourt on the country roads and reached St. Quentin-de-Pres in around an hour. It was actually more of a mingling of farm houses than a town. There were a few people milling around at sunset and we got better directions from them. We arrived at Madame Simone's bed and breakfast as night was setting in.

Madame Simone's was a compound of three buildings. A barn to the left and houses to the right and center. In the muddy courtyard in the middle were three wild boxers who kept us from entering the gate. After putting the dogs in the barn, we were welcomed by Madam Simone's husband Robert. We stored our bikes in the barn and walked to the house. Robert was not what we expected. He was about forty years old and a retired engineer who taught bridge and played in tournaments over the internet. He wore a pullover V-neck sweater. We expected a farmer in overalls. He led us to our room. It was a nicely remodeled area of the visitors house. And it had a shower with good pressure and lots of hot water. While fighting for the right to shower first, we found our backpacks were wet inside and out. We had to unpack everything and lay all our clothes on every available piece of furniture, windowsill, wall heater and ceiling beam to let them dry. While I was in the shower, Karen went downstairs to see if she could borrow a hair drier. When I finally got the chill out of my body and got out of the shower Karen was sitting on the side of the bed. Her complexion was white. "I'm not eating here. I looked in the kitchen and the counters were covered with bones and feathers, blood and dirty dishes." It was a mess and she couldn't find anyone to ask about a hair drier either. After a warm shower and clean, albeit damp clothes I convinced her to come down to the dining room.

We were the first two people down stairs in the dining room. On the table was a mound of hard bread under a towel and several decanters of wine. Robert came in with his young daughter, Chloe, who was about eight years old. He informed us that Madame Simone would not be cooking tonight. She just got back from the hospital where she had a vein stripping procedure and had to stay in bed. "But don't worry, dinner will be ready shortly".

Two of the full time borders then came down to the dining room. In our best French and English, I learned they were in their late twenties and worked at the airbag factory in the town of Gournay-en-Bray. When I asked if there were any other borders they snickered. Evidently, a young woman, Fabian, also lived there. Both borders said she is too aggressive in her job and she also tries to impress people by how well she is doing. They often made fun of her behind her back. Finally Robert entered with the entree. I could see a large female figure through the edge of the kitchen door. Was it Madame Simone? The entree was uncovered and a large baked chicken was unveiled. I could see in Karen's eyes that was what was in the kitchen and her thinking "I'm not eating it." Actually it wasn't too bad and with plenty of potatoes and wine we had a pleasant dinner.

Halfway through dinner Fabian arrived. The borders chuckled "Bonsoir." She walked around the table and gave everyone a kiss on the cheek except for me. She filled her plate and sat down. After a few minutes of idle table chatter Karen turned to her and innocently asked, "So how was your day?" With that generic question she stood up and yelled, "Not good!" and ran out of the house crying and drove away. We never saw her again. The borders couldn't keep from laughing. Robert looked at us. "I think it is boy troubles." We finished dinner without Fabian or the mysterious Madam Simone.

MONET'S ENVIRONS

The next morning was cool and sunny. Our clothes were damp but not uncomfortable to wear. We had a hearty breakfast of cheeses and bread. We said goodbye to the borders, except Fabian who never returned last night, and Monsieur Simone and rode out of the courtyard through the farmlands of St. Quentin-de-Pres.

The roads were narrow and gravelly as we approached Gournay-en-Bray. The traffic got busier as we approached the industrial town. We were soon on a busy two lane highway heading south. After contending with trucks for a while out of Gournay, we pulled into a charming French bakery or patisserie in the village of Neuf-Marche. The aromas of freshly baked bread hit us as we walked in the door. Everything in the shop was right out of the oven. We selected an apple tart and a chocolate croissant for starters and for good measure a coconut muffin that resembled a giant macaroon. We motioned to the clerk with three fingers for our order. We took our booty and got on our bikes to find a spot to enjoy the pastries. We found a little bench on the side of the road.

On reaching into the bag we found the clerk gave us three of the large, coconut muffins. They were all delicious and we ate the extra muffins throughout the day.

We rode on toward the town of Gisors. We encountered a driving hailstorm while riding on D915. The small ice pellets stung our faces until we were forced to pull over. We found shelter at a covered bus stop. We nibbled on the muffins till the storm subsided. In Gisors we stopped for lunch in a tiny café. The hot vegetable soup helped us warm up and again we hung out our jackets and rainwear over the radiators to dry out during lunch. We noticed a poster on the wall behind us advertising imported California wines. It seemed ironic in this area with an abundance of inexpensive French wines

After lunch we set out on a delightful route for bicycling. On leaving Gisors, we were soon on a very quiet road paralleling the Epte river. This river is a tributary of the Seine and is a location for many Impressionistic paintings. It flow just southeast of Giverny and painters from the art colony used this stretch of the river as a subject for their landscapes. We rode through farmlands filled with the bright yellow flowers of rape plants. There were chateaus high on the bluffs across the river from us. Although it was drizzling again, we found a public path down to a tiny arched bridge over the river. The water was high and flowing very rapidly underneath us as we sat in the middle of the bridge. We finished what was left of our coconut pastries. It was utterly hypnotic sitting in the soft rain over the rushing water.

Relaxing over the Epte River

We eventually got back on the road and headed toward La Roche-Guyon. We took a ninety degree turn to the west and crossed the Epte and headed toward Giverny. We arrived there about 6 P.M. as the twilight was falling. There was no big signs announcing the town made famous by Claude Monet. There were just the normal highway markers and a sign announcing the times for mass at the local church.

We rode uphill from the main road and entered a village that seemed to have stopped in time. We rode down the central street, rue Claude Monet. On each side were old stones houses used as art galleries and studios for Monet wannabes. We only saw one or two restaurants. Everything else, except the modern American Museum, remained as it was during the time of Monet. It was now dusk. All the tourists on day trips were gone. The parking lots were rid of the large tourist buses. Only a few people were meandering down the middle of the road. There was no automobile traffic. We rode past the Hotel Baude where many artists lived while working in the 19th century. It's mustard yellow exterior looks like the original paint. The high windows on the first floor café let ample light into room that was a studio for the artists of that time. Further down the ancient church overhangs the road with its old cemetery around the back. The whole village is maybe 4 or 5 blocks long. Monet's house is on the north side of the street although it wouldn't be recognized as anything special from the road. But upon entering, you would discover the famous gardens and ponds. The water lilies and the arched bridge are there also. It is kept very much as it was in Monet's lifetime.

A few blocks west of Monet's house we went into a bed and breakfast. On inquiring about openings, they said they were fully booked. She suggested we try Les Rouges Gorges in the next block. We talked to the proprietors, Eric and Christelle Carriere, and found they had one room left in the loft of the guest house. It was perfect for Giverny. It was an old stone house across from the main building. There were two rooms up the stairs with a shared bathroom. The main floor looked like an old storage space for farm equipment. It was where breakfast was served in the morning. The yard had a table set up for outdoor dining and there were a multitude of cats and kittens milling around. To make things ideal, I asked Christelle if they would like to buy our bikes from us. I thought that would be a nice option for their guests. She didn't comprehend what I was saying but fortunately an Englishman fluent in French was standing next to me. He explained what I was suggesting and we exchanged our bikes as payment for our evening lodging. As we were unpacking our duffle bags we saw Christelle and her twin sister ride down rue Claude Monet on their new bikes. With our bikes gone, we realized the first leg of our journey had come to an end.

Leg Two:
Giverny to Poitiers
April, 2004

RETURN TO GIVERNY

The sun was shining as we attached our panniers to our bikes. That was a good omen since weather.com called for a 90% chance of rain. We were back in Giverny after a three year wait to continue our journey across France.

So far we've been fortunate to get to this point. Our late arrival the previous day at Charles de Gaulle airport put us behind schedule. We made a quick trip from the airport to the Gare St. Lazare on the RER rail system into Paris. A short three block walk took us to the UPS office. This is where we planned to ship our suitcase to our final destination in Poitiers. The only problem was no one, either in the U.S. or France, told us that the suitcase had to be boxed for shipping. The proprietor at UPS said they didn't have boxes big enough at their office to hold the suitcase. She suggested looking at a stationery store a few blocks away. I left Karen in the office and took off down the street to the store. Upon finding the store I waited in various lines to ask about buying a box. Again, they didn't have one big enough for the troublesome suitcase. I noticed a large packing box not yet unloaded and asked if they would sell it to me but again the answer was "No." They did say the post office might have one. Another two block hike got me to La Poste. I was able to communicate to the clerk what I needed and she said they could mail it directly to Poitiers if it was wrapped and not over weight. I thanked her and hurried back to the UPS office. Of course, Karen was worrying about me since I was gone for almost an hour. We gathered up our luggage and trekked to La Poste again. The suitcase passed the weight requirement. Now all we had to do was wrap it since even brown paper covering would be sufficient. A quick walk down the street took us to an office supply store. We bought three sheets of brown paper and a roll of wrapping tape. Back at the post office we used a corner of the building to wrap and tape the suitcase. It now fit the requirements to be mailed. The clerk took it from us and "voila" it was on its way to Poitiers. Incidentally, the cost was one sixth of what the UPS rate would have been. At last we were ready to head on to Giverny.

Now we walked back to Gare St. Lazare. We waited about 45 minutes for a train to Vernon, the nearest stop to the village of Giverny. We were tired and dozed a little on the hour and a half trip but we were awake enough to enjoy the views of the Seine.

We arrived at Vernon right at 5PM. I knew the bike shop was located at #10 Carnot. I didn't know how far it was or how late it remained open. We were anticipating arriving several hours earlier. We jumped in a taxi and rode only a few blocks to the shop. Fortunately, most businesses stay open until 7PM on weekdays. Eyeing the limited supply of bicycles, we did find two that fit our needs. Both were 18 speed hybrids with luggage racks. Karen's was a Gitane and mine was a MBK. The price was fair enough and Karen talked him into a 5% volume discount. The shop owner was nice enough to give us a lift to Giverny, about two and a half kilometers away, and then deliver the bikes that evening when he had a truck available. Thus, we accomplished our preliminary tasks on our arrival day so we could leave early the next morning.

We stayed at a remodeled Giverny farm house B&B called Le Clos Fleuri. The proprietress, Danielle Fouche, was a talkative French woman who grew up in Australia so language was no problem. She moved back to France some twenty-five years ago. She and her husband bought the property and he commuted to his engineering job outside of Paris. Gradually, they turned it into a B&B as interest in Giverny and Monet's legacy increased. It was just down a hill from Rue Claude Monet, the main street of Giverny. When we arrived Rue Claude Monet was deserted. It usually is in the evenings but awash with tourists during the day. That evening we took a leisurely stroll down Rue Claude Monet, past the American Museum and Monet's house, to the only restaurant open that spring evening. We enjoyed crepes and wine and wound down from a very long and busy day of travel. In any event, we were ready to head south in the morning.

GIVERNY TO CHARTRES

It was down the rue Claude Monet that we began our journey to the south on the sunny April morning. Our bikes were efficiently packed and our raincoats were ready for use. We said adieu to Danielle and glided away from Les Clos Fleuri.

Riding down rue Claude Monet, we passed the ochre colored Hotel Baudi where many of Monet's contemporaries lived and worked in the 1890's. Further down the road we passed the pink building where Monet lived during his most creative period. From the road we could just get a glimpse of the gardens that were immortalized in so many of his paintings. Shortly, we were out of the village and heading east on D5 in the French countryside.

What can I say about our first day riding? We waited three years to continue this route. I looked at maps for years and wondered what the roads and terrain would be like. Well, it was all I could have hoped for. The sky was bright blue and almost cloudless. We shortly turned south and headed toward the Seine. We crossed branches of the Epte River. Monet received permission from the Giverny city council in the 1890's to divert these branches of the river to nourish his immortal garden. We rode across an oxbow made from a bend in the Seine river. Within five miles we were crossing the winding Seine from Bennecourt to Bonnieres-sur-Seine. The river is quite wide at this point and we could see factories lining the shores in either direction. It was a steep climb leaving the bank on the south side. It was probably the steepest climb of the whole trip. We left Bonnieres, crossed under the A13 expressway and were in rolling fields for the rest of the day. Our goal was Chartres but we weren't sure it was realistic. The riding here was delightful. We spent several hours on D89. It was a fairly quiet route. The scenery was composed of rolling hills and farms. We passed through towns Menil-Guyon and Breval. At Gilles we rode through the Foret de Guainville to La Chaussee d'Ivry. This section took us out of the farmlands into a forested landscape. I promised Karen when we reached the fold on our map page we would stop for lunch. This took us to the town of Bu. In Bu we found a boulangerie for baguettes and a boucherie for ham and cheese. There was even a patisserie for macaroons. Behind the shops was an abandoned mill with the remains of a waterwheel dipping in the slowly flowing river. Most of the windows were broken and pigeons inhabited the window sills. We climbed down to the edge of the water and sat with our feet dangling in the water. We lunched beneath the old watermill.

From Bu we headed straight south on D21 to Coulombs. Here we had our first opportunity to follow a route along a river. The river we paralleled was the Eure, a tributary of the Seine. We would follow it all the way to Chartres. In Coulombs it was crossed by a lovely bridge lined on each side by evenly spaced poplars. We then shortly had to cross back over a more generic bridge since we wanted to remain on the east side of the river. This kept us on a quieter road, the D116, heading south. We followed the Eure to Maintenon. Maintenon had a picturesque chateaux overlooking the river. We were tempted to stop but knew we still had a ways to go if we were to get to Chartres that day. We crossed to the west side of the Eure at Maintenon and followed the busier D6. We had beautiful views of the river as we climbed the bluffs along the way. As we passed St. Prest the road was getting crowded. As we looked to the south over the flat plains below, we could see the outline of the magnificent Chartres Cathedral rising in the distance. We approached the city in some traffic and passed the small airport and soccer stadium. As we entered Chartres we rode downhill to the Eure river. As we crossed the river, we could see the half-timbered buildings of medieval tanneries and mills. Flower and vegetable gardens filled the small islands in the river. We soon realized we were in a bustling city with a lot of traffic. By now it was about six PM. The traffic was heavy at the stoplights as people hurried home. While waiting at a red light we noticed a walkway catty-corner from us. We made our way through the intersection to check it out. It was a nice pedestrian walkway that went up a hill, above the crowded streets, and became part of a path on the old ramparts around the city. As we followed it around the city we could look over the old defensive walls into the houses that had been standing there for centuries. We found signs leading to the information center. This lead us along narrow, cobbled streets to the office on the cathedral square. Inside we were given the names and addresses of several Bed & Breakfasts nearby. We walked our bikes in front of the magnificent cathedral and went looking for the B & B's. We descended down a long, narrow street away from the square. The houses lined the edge of the street and were an archaic appearing tone of gray. We knocked on the door of the first house on our list. There was no response. A few doors down we knocked at #82 Muret. Soon a woman answered. She spoke a little English. Her name was Anna and she said she just got back into town but they did have a room available. She asked us to come and relax in the living room. She seemed anxious for us to stay. We put our bicycles inside the front anteroom with her family's own bikes. Their living room was a large space combining dining and lounging areas with a high two-storied beamed ceiling. It was eclectically furnished with an old oak dining table, an iron wood burning stove, many non-matching easy chairs and many modern floor stand CD holders. The beams and wall timbers were lined with toy soldiers and farm animals. Our hostess's husband, Jean Loupe, then joined us in the circularly arranged chairs. We told him how we rode from Giverny that morning. He then got out his photo album to show us his journeys. Every summer he walks on hiking paths from Chartres to Orleans along the river trails. He hikes alone for ten days and has taken the same path over eight times. He pointed out the chateaus, cathedrals and nuclear power plants he passes each year. Interestingly, we followed the start of Jean Loupe's trek when we rode out of Chartres the next morning.

Anna entered the living room and said our room was ready. We carried our panniers up a metal spiral staircase in the corner of the large room. On the second floor landing was the bathroom with a view of their tiny garden. It was very green and lush and surrounded by high ivy-covered walls making a triangle with the back of the house. One more floor up was our room at the front of the house. To get to it we had to pass through their personal religious shrine room. In the center was an altar on an oriental rug. On the wall were banners, religious images and an oxen yoke. Our room overlooked the drab houses across the narrow Rue de Muret. It seemed like we could lean out of our window and touch their facades. Double beds with overly soft mattresses and a writing table were the extent of the room's furnishings.

After cleaning up we walked along the river Eure past the old mills. By now it was close to nine o'clock. We went to Le Tres Lillies across from the river. It was a small bistro and we ordered crepes with butter, bacon and cheese. We knew we would enjoy our chocolate dessert crepe for dessert.

We walked back to our B&B through the old town. We climbed the very steep stairways or tertres that rose from the river. We passed the cathedral and headed down Rue de Muret to get a good nights sleep after our first, long day of cycling.

CHARTRES
TO CHATEAUDUN

Today we visited the Chartres Cathedral. Since we were able to complete the trip from Giverny in one day, we had the luxury of visiting Chartres all morning. Anna served us the standard French B&B breakfast of a baguette, a croissant, jelly and butter with coffee or tea. The morning weather was brisk and clear. We walked from the house to the river. We climbed the steep tertres from the Eure river up to the Eglise de St. Andre. It is a beautiful Romanesque church overshadowed by the cathedral. Behind the churchyard were levels of terraced gardens overlooking the river. The cathedral at Chartres is considered by some the finest gothic cathedral in Europe. It was named a World Heritage Site in 1979. The original Romanesque cathedral was built in 1020 and burned down in 1194. Amazingly, it took only 25 years for the lords and peasants of Chartres to rebuild the present structure. Probably the most outstanding feature of the cathedral is the miraculous 150 stained glass windows that depict not only biblical themes but daily activities of the 13th century.

The windows were donated by the royalty and merchant guilds in the early 1200's. The inside of the cathedral is magnificent. The clarity and colors of the stained glass is breathtaking. We followed the audio route around the cathedral that explained the topic of each window. On a day that would eventually be very mild, the temperature and dampness inside was bone-chilling. As the tour led us out of the building to view the carvings of the Royal Portico and South Porch, we wished we had brought heavier coats.

We felt the next task should be to find something warm to drink. We walked through the pedestrian streets and found a little bistro with a fireplace. We sat at a corner table and enjoyed hot tea and hot chocolate. After getting some warmth back in our bodies, we walked back to the rue Muret along the hilltop ramparts.

Leaving Chartres

On returning back to the B&B, we changed into our biking clothes and packed up our panniers. We bid adieu to Anna on the cobblestones outside her front door. We left about 1:30pm and were soon crossing a humpbacked stone bridge over the Eure. We had gone only ten minutes when Karen's pedals starting rubbing her panniers. We had to pull into a parking area and remove and reposition all her packs. We finally were on our way to continue south. We found Jean Loupe's hiking path out of the city. It followed the Eure river at the edge of a large city park. It soon led to our route heading south and we joined a busy route D935. In the town of Dammarie we were able to turn onto a much quieter country road. We had a very pleasant ride that afternoon to our destination of Chateaudun. We rode down the long, straight D127 until we reach Godonville. There we turned to the west and crossed the Conie River, not much bigger than a creek. We rode through the forest Bois de Moleans. There are many grenouilleries, or frog farms, in this area. They serenaded us with their croaking as we cycled past.

As we neared Chateaudun, the road got much busier and we road uphill to where we had a panoramic view overlooking the town. In the distance we could see the Chateau Chateaudun. The town was built around this fortress on the Loir River (not Loire). We rode into the town square and found the information office. They suggested the Hotel St. Michael across the square. The town square had a small park with a large World War II monument in the center. However, most of the square was occupied by a parking lot. We walked across the square and booked a room. The hotel had a covered atrium where we could lock up our bikes. The room on the second floor was small and clean. It had a large picture window looking onto the atrium. After unpacking and changing clothes we walked down to the Loir River to see the chateau before it got dark. We went down a very steep stairway overlooking the gardens of the small houses along the river. About a quarter of a mile walk took us to the chateau. Standing on the river bank, the castle rose dramatically in front of us. It's vertical wall rose straight up eighty feet. It looked like the impenetrable fortress it was designed to be. The castle was originally from the tenth century. The Earl of Dunois rebuilt it to its present appearance between 1451 and 1468. Walking back up the steep hill, we circled the front of the chateau and walked down narrow ancient streets back to the town square. We had dinner at a busy restaurant, Le Licorne or the Unicorn. It was nicely decorated with fresh flowers on each table. After dinner we walked around the square. We concluded the evening with a bottle of wine at an outdoor table at the brasserie next to the Hotel St. Michael.

ALONG THE LOIR

We awoke to another crisp, sunny day. Looking from our window into the atrium, I was happy to see our bikes were still where we were asked to leave them. We went through the ritual of packing our clothes in plastic bags and stuffing them into our panniers. We then carried them downstairs and attached them onto the luggage racks. With our bikes, we walked around the square to the boulangerie and epicerie (separate stores for baked goods and groceries). The stores were crowded with customers stocking up with food for the day. We purchased croissants, baguettes, yogurt and fresh fruit. We had breakfast on a bench in the town square under the WW11 commemorative monument. The flowers decorating the square were moist and beautiful at this time of the morning.

After finishing breakfast, we rode out of Chateaudun first on fairly busy, city streets and then on the high speed N10 highway. After a few miles, we were able to turn off onto our road heading south, the D145. We were now into flat farmlands on very quiet, narrow country roads. We rode through acres of rapeseed plants with their bright yellow flowers shining in the sunlight. After about an hour in the fields, we rode downhill to the Loir valley at Bouche d'Aigre. We were soon in bicycling Nirvana. We followed the banks of the Loir on a quiet riverside road. At times there were beautiful chateaus behind high walls with ornate iron gates. We could see other stately chateaus across the Loir. There were families with tiny plots of land on the banks set with tables and chairs. Some groups were fishing while other were visiting and just enjoying the view. Swans were swimming in the shallow water along the banks. We noticed many houses had yellow bags in their windows or mailboxes. We inspected one and found out they were bakery deliveries. They were getting their freshly baked baguettes delivered right to their door. We eventually caught up to the delivery truck. We waved down the driver and asked her if she had any baguettes to sell. She did have extra baguettes with her. When we received the bread we were so excited that we forgot to pay her and started to ride off. We looked back and she had this bewildered look about her. We went back and paid her and apologized as well as we could in French. We took our baguettes and water bottles and found a nice spot to sit along the river to have our midmorning snack. Trucks delivering baguettes! What a place!

We left our quiet, riverside road at Hilaire-Gravelle and turned onto the busy D19 toward Moree. We soon were paralleling the Loir again but this time on a crowded national route. We could see families enjoying their outings at their retreats along the river. We rode along the eastern bank of the Loir through Meslay and crossed over an old stone bridge into the town of Vendome. The old city of Vendome is set on an island in the Loir. The town square is encircled by half-timbered buildings housing brassieries and restaurants. There were throngs of people sitting at outdoor tables. It was a perfect setting for a Saturday afternoon of leisure. A statue of American Revolutionary hero Rochambeau, a native of Vendome, overlooks the center of the square. We bought baguettes filled with cheese and ham and grabbed an empty bench in the square for our late lunch. We walked around the stores, looked in at the Abbe church of La Trinite with its flamboyant gothic tracery and original Romanesque bell tower. We visited the pasterie shop for afternoon sustenance. As we rode away Karen realized she left her sunglasses on the bench so we quickly turned back to see if we could find it. While inspecting the area around the bench, a young man across the square came over and asked if we had left a pair of sunglasses on the bench and returned them to us. We gave him many "mercies" for finding them. We rode out through the old south gate and we headed uphill away from the river. We could hear a marching band in the distance, a part of the weekend activities of the town.

We were soon again on very quiet roads through farm villages such as Chantelloup, Sasnieres, and Villechauve on route D67. We played skip-across with the TVG train tracks as we crossed its overpasses three times. These overpasses were probably the steepest climbs we'd had in several days. We stopped under a blossoming cherry tree in Neuville-Brenne to check our maps on our way to Chateau-Renault. We were fortunate to be traveling when so many trees were in full bloom. We finished the macaroons we bought in Vendome while resting there. By now it was early evening and our goal for the day was not far off. We entered Chateau-Renault on a rather busy highway and went directly to the town square. The information office was closed by the time we arrived but there were names of hotels in its window. We found a map of the town in the square and headed to Rue de Victor Hugo where several hotels were located. We drifted downhill on a busy but narrow street. The first hotel was in a dingy building and we elected to skip it. It was surprising to see so few people on the narrow sidewalks. A few blocks further we got to the Hotel Lyon d'Or. Standing outside, Karen declared this hotel would be fine. All the windows had window boxes planted with fresh flowers. Inside we were greeted by the clerk. In poor English, he said there was a room available and a garage for our bikes. We elected to stay for dinner in their dining room. We took our bikes around the corner and entered a courtyard through a big wooden gate.

We put our bikes in a garage space and locked them to a drain pipe. We went in the backdoor to shower and change for dinner.

On coming down to in the dining room we found the clerk did more than work the desk. He was also the cook, busboy and I wouldn't be surprised if he cleaned the rooms as well. We were seated in the dining room. The room had a pleasant wood-paneled décor. Our table looked onto the street over a geranium filled window box. Surprisingly, there was no one else eating there.

Our waitress came over to take our order. Ordering off a French menu, we had a lot of questions. She spoke very little English and went to get the jack-of-all-trades clerk. He was trying to answer our questions but excused himself from our table before he was finished taking our order. No one come back for five or ten minutes. We were wondering what had happened when another young woman come over. She spoke English quite well and said she was Michelle, the clerk's wife. When they couldn't communicate with us, he called her at home to come to the hotel to take our order. Needless to say, we enjoyed our dinner and wine and the hospitality at the Hotel Lyon d'Or.

ON TO TOURS

We planned for an easy day of riding leaving Chateau-Renault. Or so we thought.

We only had twenty or twenty-five miles to our next destination. Our plan was to arrive in Tours by two o'clock. We had breakfast in the hotel before leaving. The hard working clerk Michael was surprisingly not on duty. We packed our bikes and rode uphill on the Rue de la Republic and headed south. We rode the busy D46 to Neuille-le-Lierre on the Brenne River, a tributary of the Loire River. After only riding an hour and a half we felt like stopping for an early lunch. The only place in Neuille that was open was the All-Star Café, a sort of French sports bar. We asked them to make our standard fare of ham and cheese on baguettes to go. They gladly agreed and we crossed the small town to the bank of the river Brenne. While we ate we watched fishermen upstream cast their lines in the water. We watched horseback riders at an equestrian center across the river. We figured we had plenty of time to get to Tours by early afternoon. According to our map, there was a quiet road on the east side of the river. We left the more direct, busier D46 and crossed the bridge over the Brenne. We turned south and bicycled on a sparsely used road that followed the edge of the river. It first went through a formal park with athletic fields and a swimming pool. It then led into a quiet forest that lined the eastern bank of the river. Later on we noticed a chateau, Chateau de Valmer, up the hill to the west. It appeared to be a winery. We decided to investigate but on riding on the long driveway uphill toward the building, we noted it was not open to the public for another week. We did see a line of Citroen automobiles lined up waiting to go into the courtyard. Our curiosity was aroused and we continued riding to the chateau. We found a cameraman at the gate and he told us they were doing a documentary about Citroen automobiles. We watched the filming of the classic autos driving into the gates of Chateau Valmer and even shared a glass of wine with the crew.

We crossed back over the Brenne River and rode west. We were trying to avoid riding on the highway along the Loire River. We figured if we rode directly north of Tours we could find a safer route into the city. Across the Brenne from Chateau Valmer is the town of Chancay and we left the small town in the direction of La Vaux. Now this is where our map skills got challenged. After riding through a tiny village surrounded by vineyards our road came to a dead end. We reversed our route back to D46 near Chancay and followed another sign to La Vaux. After riding too long without finding La Vaux, we began to wonder if this was also the wrong way. I saw a sign to Monnaie. I looked this up in my dictionary and saw that it was a mint or a bank. I told Karen it was just a sign to a bank or maybe an ATM. After another 45 minutes we neared the A10 Expressway. I know this was not on our route. I checked the map again. This time, I saw a town, Monnaie, not a mint, and realized we were going back north. A sign at a crossroad directed us straight south on D47 to Vouvray on the Loire River. This was the type of road we were trying to avoid all along. We rode hard with a purpose to get ourselves back on track. A half hour later we reached Vouvray and stopped at a lovely outdoor brasserie. Here we could relax in the mid afternoon and try to figure out how I could have gotten turned in the wrong direction. A cold Pepsi and crepe under the maroon umbrellas helped ease the pain of the extra miles.

We then headed west along the mighty Loire River on a busy two-lane road. It had a fairly wide shoulder so it wasn't too crowded riding the six miles to Tours. The view of the river was refreshing to look at while we cycled. There were several parks next to the river. On the north side of the road were vineyards and occasionally a chateau on the bluffs above us. We passed an amusement park with merry-go-rounds and a Ferris wheel. As we neared Tours the traffic got heavier. We had to find a bridge to cross the river. The first roundabout we came to only gave directions to Samor or Orleans, towns on the Loire River but dozens of miles away. We kept going straight and found a sign to Tours that led up to an expressway. We continued further and a sign said, "Leaving Tours." We were at an impasse. I didn't want to make another mistake and head in the wrong direction a second time. I guessed we needed to take the expressway bridge over the river. We started in that direction up the steep ramp. Several cars honked and warned us not to go that way. So we turned around again and headed downhill to the east. We arrived back at the first turnabout and decided to follow it west. We soon realized that was where we needed to be all along since it was the continuation of N152, the road from Vouvray. We soon found a bridge entrance on a busy road, but certainly not expressway busy, over the Loire. We later learned if we had gone only a little farther there was a pedestrian only bridge which would have taken us into the center of the city.

We rode across the river into Tours. We could see the twin spires of St. Gatien Cathedral, with its dark Gothic façade, near the southern bank. There were biking and jogging paths along the south side of the river. Tours is the capital of the Indre-et-Loire Department. It is a university town with a long history back to Roman times. It was the capital of France in the 15th century. On reaching the town, we got out our map of Tours and began to look for hotels. I made a list of half a dozen hotels in the old part of town from guide books I studied before our trip. We walked our bikes through the narrow streets of Rue Colbert and Rue de la Scellerie near the river. We passed the Gouin Mansion, a former silk merchants house now an archaeology museum. Each hotel listed was either full, too crusty or closed. We decided to go to the tourist information center. We left the narrow streets of the old town and rode south on Rue Nationale, a street lined with shops and larger department stores, to the Place Jean Jaures. Here Tours took on a more cosmopolitan appearance. The Place Jean Jaures was planted with shrubbery and blooming flowers. The city hall and court buildings were designed in elegant 19th century architecture. The train station was a beautiful art deco structure designed by Victor Laloux, who also designed the Gare de Orsay, now the Museum de Orsay in Paris. The wide boulevards Beranger and Heurteloup ran west and east from Place Jean Jaures.

The tourist office was situated across from the train station. They were able to recommend a hotel a few blocks down Boulevard Heurteloup or turtle soup as I liked to call it. The boulevard had a central sidewalk and it made a nice three block ride to the Hotel Mirabeau. The hotel had a stone exterior with large windows and wrought iron gates outside. We entered the slightly ornate doorway and met Mme. Dubon. She showed us to our room and led us to a courtyard where our bikes could be kept. We saw her at all times of the day; serving breakfast, supervising the staff or working the front desk.

Our room had twelve foot high ceilings with windows opening to the Boulevard. In a corner was an interesting compartment surrounded with opaque glass that housed the sink and step-down shower. It had the best water pressure we had in France. The furniture was old mahogany but comfortable and well maintained.

After resting a while, we walked to a laundromat. We packed enough clothes in our panniers to last four days and we planned on doing a wash in Tours. We got directions for a laundromat about three blocks away. We stuffed our clothes into the panniers and took all the coins we had. When we got there we had no idea how to begin. All instructions were of course in French. There were no coin slots on any of the machines. We asked a young man who was reading while waiting for his wash how to work the machines. With no knowledge of English, he showed us the depository for the coins that controlled all the machines. It was located in a far corner of the store. You had to punch in which machine you were going to use and how long you wanted it to run. Then you had to put in the appropriate amount of coins. After getting detergent and starting our white and dark loads, we knew we wouldn't have enough change. However, there was no bill changer in the store. I went looking for change and shortly came to one of the omnipresent bakeries. I bought a chocolate croissant with a ten Euro bill. This gave me plenty of change or so I thought. By the time I returned, Karen was loading the dryers. The dryers ate all our remaining change by running for the six shortest minutes I can remember. With our change dwindling and our clothes still damp another trip to the boulangerie was necessary for some large macaroons plus change. After a few more cycles in the dryers, we had our clothes clean and dry and our appetites gone.

That evening we walked to the medieval center of Tours called Place Plumereau. Its narrow streets are lined with cafes, galleries and boutiques. We first went to an internet café and e-mailed home for the first time since arriving in France. It was comforting to hear all was well there. By then our appetites had revived enough to enjoy dinner at one of the outdoor tables at a popular bistro. After dinner we wandered back to the Hotel Mirabeau and slept well after a long, tiring day that was supposed to be a short one.

We decided not to continue south the next day. Instead we visited two beautiful chateaus in the Loire Valley, d'Azay-de-le-Rideou and Villandry. Chateau d'Azay-le-Rideau is about seven miles west of Tours. The castle sits on an island in the middle of the Indre river. Built in the XVIth century by Gilles Berthelot, it is a perfect combination of Gothic style with fairy tale decorations. With a drawbridge over a reflecting pool and pointed turrets on all corners, it certainly appears to be the pleasure palace it was designed to be.

On our way back to Tours we stopped at Chateau de Villandry. It is a much more imposing structure built in the Henry IV style. It has an almost vertical appearance without the frills of Azay-de-le-Rideau. The real charm of Villandry is its gardens. There are formal, terraced gardens in perfect geometric designs. We walked through the ornamental gardens depicting different qualities of love, such as tender or tragic. The water gardens were on a raised terrace to the south. We circled through the herb gardens and kitchen gardens. Karen, being an amateur gardener herself, was hyperventilating as we strolled through the vegetables in the kitchen garden arranged in perfect geometric designs. She tried valiantly to discuss gardening with the workers meticulously tending the vegetables.

Gardens of Chateau Villandry

We got back to Tours late in the afternoon. We wandered in the old part of the city and visited Cathedral St. Gatien. On returning to the hotel Mme. Dubon was at work at the front desk as usual.

THROUGH THE TOURAINE

The next morning we were raring to get started after not traveling for a day. We packed our panniers and went down to the breakfast room. Our bikes were right outside the window in the small courtyard. After we finished our croissant and baguette breakfast, we had to wheel our bikes through the maze of tables and chairs filled with travelers. We packed the panniers on our bikes on the marble floor in the front entrance hall. I gave Madam Dubon a big hug as we left the hotel.

We rode on Boulevard Heurteloup a few blocks until we saw a grocery store. We stopped so Karen could refill our supply of water and snacks. From there we rode south on very crowded city streets until we reached the park on the banks of the Cher River. Tours is actually set between the Loire and Cher Rivers, which then join together several miles to the west. We found the narrow pedestrian bridge over the Cher River which took us to another park on the Isle d'Balzac. A second pedestrian bridge took us to the south bank of the river which was lined by another park with paths along the Cher. We headed west. This was a beautiful way to leave a large city. The paths took us up to the busy D86 bridge and we turned south through Joue-Les-Tours. We followed it until we reached another Loire tributary, the Indre River. We turned toward the village of Artannes-sur-Indre and followed the river west along its north bank. At the village of Sache, we crossed the river again near an ancient stone water wheel. On the south edge of town we stopped to visit the Chateau de Sache. It is a stately manor converted from a feudal castle. The Chateau is known as the temporary residence of Honore de Balzac, the noted 19th century French author. While avoiding Parisian creditors, Balzac lived here from 1830 to 1837 as a guest of Monsieur de Margonne. It is in the little second floor room that he wrote parts of his greatest masterpieces. It has a lovely but modest garden surrounding the house. We relaxed in the gardens after touring the house.

Chateau de Sache

We left Sache and headed south on an unmarked road. This always made me nervous because you can find yourself a long way off course before figuring out your location. After about twenty minutes we merged with D8 and knew we were headed in the right direction. We spent about an hour on quiet roads through the Foret, or forest, De Crissay. At Trogues we joined D109 on the east bank of the Vienne River, another tributary of the Loire. We followed it south to Pouzay and crossed over the river and followed its west bank the next fifteen miles to Chatellerault, our day's destination. The road was along a hilly ridge which gave us great views of the Vienne and its valley.

We entered Chatellerault over an ornate 16th century bridge across the Vienne River. A short turn through a flower-filled park took us to the main street. We rode a few blocks to the visitors center. We got a couple of hotel recommendations and headed to the nearby Hotel del University. I waited on the street with the bikes while Karen went up to inspect the rooms. When she came down she pulled me aside and told me there was no way we would be staying in that hotel. The smell from the bathroom was overwhelming. We excused ourselves and headed to our next choice. Hotel Gresko was on a side street over a bistro. The proprietress took us up to the room. It was scary but Karen didn't want to search anymore. Besides, it was an improvement from the Hotel del University. So we overnighted at Hotel Gresko.

There was a side entrance with a narrow hallway where we stored our bikes. The room had no TV and no clock. The bedspread looked like it was from WWII. There was one rickety chair. We took our showers down the hall. But it only cost $22 for the night including breakfast, so we toughened it out.

After changing our clothes we walked down the main street. It was very quiet with very few people out. A few teenagers were skateboarding in the center parking lot. After walking both ways on the street we went to one of the brasseries that was still open. We both had omelets for dinner. Afterwards we walked through the narrow streets behind our hotel looking for the chateau of Chatellerault but we never did find it. We were quite tired after biking fifty miles that day so we gave up our search and returned to the Hotel Gresko for the night.

THE HOMESTRETCH
TO POITIERS

The next morning we were anxious to pack up and leave. The atmosphere of the hotel did not warrant remaining any longer than necessary. We elected not to partake in breakfast in the bar downstairs. We rolled our bikes out of the narrow hallway and put the panniers on outside on the sidewalk across the street. We waved adieu to the Hotel Gresko and rode out to the main street and turned right past the brasserie from the previous night. We made a quick stop at the epicurie or grocery store just down the street to load up with water and baguettes for lunch. We stopped for a few minutes at a busy outdoor market selling fruits and vegetables, meats and clothing. We took the road toward the local airport and then crossed the Vienne River near its merge with the Clain River at the town of Netbuis. We rode south between the two rivers following the Clain to the west. Near Vieux-Poitiers we stopped for a few minutes at a Roman excavation. We watched the few workers do their painstakingly slow digging in trenches. There was a Roman theater in amazing condition. There were towers 40-50 feet high around what was once the theater's walls. Back on the road we found ourselves riding along a golf course as we approached St. Cyr. We took a look inside the clubhouse to compare it to our courses back home.

We continued south and rode down a long hill into the town of Dissay. As we were going down the narrow streets we could see the spires of the Chateau de Dissay over the rooftops. We didn't expect a large chateau on our route.. The chateau was a formidable, stone defensive-looking structure that was surrounded by a wide moat. The building was closed to visitors at this time. We learned it was only open on Sundays. But it was open to active bird life with swallows and flycatchers going in and out of the nooks and crannies. Birds were nesting within the broken windows on the upper levels. A chorus of frogs called from the lily pads in the moat. In the parking area a produce truck was set up to sell its wares. We bought apples and bananas to have along with our baguettes. A patisserie across the road sold desserts to go with our lunch. So we sat on the wall of the moat and had lunch under the pointed turrets of Chateau de Dissay.

We left Dissay and headed south toward our final destination of Poitiers. The roads now were hilly going up and down through woods and fields. We had reservations to stay at the Chateau de Vaumoret. But as we continued south we began questioning if we were headed in the right direction. I knew the chateau was on the outskirts of Poitiers but we were no where near anything that looked like a city. Finally, I saw a sign for the Chateau de Vaumoret.

Another kilometer down the road got us to the entrance of the Chateau de Vaumoret. A long gravel road lined on both sides with trees led us to the gate of the courtyard. We were definitely out in the country. The chateau, built in the 17th century, was located on fifteen hectares of farm and woodland. We entered the courtyard through the large iron gate. The main house was directly in front of us. There were wings on each side with the left wing being mostly stables. We knocked on the door in the center of the main building. No one answered. We opened the door and yelled inside. No one answered. Evidently no one was there. We went back out and walked around the buildings. Behind one of the wings was a furnished apartment with a half opened Dutch door. We yelled hello inside and met our first living creature on the estate, a large German shepherd dog with a huge head. We later learned his name was Goeff. We found out he had a passion for chasing tennis balls and was fortunately very friendly. But on our first encounter you wouldn't want him to be any other way. Moments later a women appeared inside the apartment. "We are the Kretchmars and have a reservation for tonight." She spoke no English but realized we were the ones who had mailed the suitcase they received. We totally forgot about that but we were relieved that the French postal service got it to the right place. I asked where Mr. Johnson, the owner, was. One reason we stayed there was because they stated English was spoken and we could correspond easily with him. But Mr. Johnson was out of town. I explained to the woman, who's name was Anne, that we had finished a long bicycle trip and needed a place for dinner and wanted to sell our bikes. Obviously there was no where around the rural chateau to eat and no one looking to buy our bikes. She got on the telephone and called an English speaking friend. I explained our dilemma to her. She knew no one who wanted our bikes even at a really good price. In all honesty, I knew the chateau was on the outskirts of Poitiers but I thought there would be some cafes and stores nearby with public transportation. We were really out in the countryside.

Chateau de Vaumoret

Soon her husband, Jonique, the estate caretaker drove his tractor back from the fields. We explained our situation again to him. He also spoke very little English. He said there was a commercial center on the outskirts of Poitiers that would buy our bikes. He got a map and started showing us directions there. I knew we would have a difficult time finding it and it was getting late in the afternoon. I was anxious to start riding again if we were going to try to sell our bikes there. We must have looked despondent. Finally, Jonique motioned for us to follow him outside. He put our bikes in his station wagon and drove us to Poitiers.

On the peripheral road surrounding Poitiers was a shopping center with several large big box stores. Our destination turned out to be a resale shop called "Easy Cash." We unloaded our bikes and went inside. We took a waiting number. There were about six people ahead of us. The wait went slowly as one of the two clerks was always in the back. People were selling boxes with dozens of toys in them or parts of their CD collections. We sat patiently for half an hour as did Jonique. I was wondering what chores he wasn't getting done.

Finally, they called our number. There was no English spoken. Jonique did our talking for us. They asked what we wanted for the bikes and we said half of our original cost or about 250 Euros. The clerk said he could give us 200 Euros. Jonique and the clerk continued to haggle and a couple of minutes later he ended up giving us 220 Euros thanks to Jonique's negotiations. I accepted that amount. We signed the appropriate papers and said adieu to our two bicycles, our mode of travel the last week, and watched them wheeled to the back of "Easy Cash."

Jonique wouldn't accept any payment for his service, not even the negotiated windfall of 20 Euros. He took us to a bus stop so we could go into central Poitiers. He headed back to Chateau de Vaumoret and we jumped on a bus and rode the peripheral highway around Poitiers. We passed modern campuses of schools and businesses. We eventually got to the old section located on a rocky promontory. We walked through the narrow streets of the medieval city. Poitiers has been inhabited for 2000 years but it is best known as the site of one of the epic battles in French history. It was here that Charles Martel repelled the Arab expansion in 732 A.D. Across from the Romanesque Notre-Dame-la-Grande, Poitier's showpiece church, we found a restaurant with a Brittany motif. The waiters wore blue striped shirts and the décor was ocean related. We ordered wine from the nearby Clermont vineyards and sat back and reflected on our journey. After dinner we took a cab the eight kilometers back to Chateau Vaumoret. A dense fog had descended over the chateau while we were gone. We sat on the ledge outside our door facing the courtyard and absorbed the misty, ethereal view of the old buildings. Our second leg came to a successful finish in the beautiful countryside surrounding Poitiers.

Leg Three: Poitiers to Bordeaux

June, 2005

RETURN TO POITIERS
AND ON TO NIORT

O ur train arrived in Poitiers at 3:45 pm after leaving
Paris earlier that day. We are getting much more
efficient in our travels through France! We were able to
mail our suitcases to Bordeaux, the final destination of
this leg's trip, from the post office located in Charles De
Gaulle airport. We then jumped on the RER local train
from the airport station and rode through Paris to Gare
Montparnasse. There we were able to catch the 1:55 pm
train to Poitiers. On arriving, we grabbed our panniers
and crossed the pedestrian bridge over the train tracks
to the old town center. It was a short walk, but it was
mostly uphill as we climbed a combination of steps and
ramps to the old, inner city.

We arrived at the Ibis Hotel, which was a modern,
neatly decorated hotel. It is part of a large chain and was
an efficient place to stay for our first night. We relaxed for
just a few minutes because we knew we had to find bikes
that afternoon if we wanted to get an early start the next

day. We had no idea where to look for bikes or where bike shops would be located in the city. After talking to several people at the hotel desk, we were told we could get bikes at a super sporting center outside the old part of the city. We walked past the landmarks of central Poitiers, past the Notre-Dame-La-Grand, a 12th century church masterpiece with its lively poitevin sculptures and geometric designed columns. We went east down Rue Jean Jaures past the Baptistrere-St-Jean, a building from the 4th Century AD. We had no time to stop and look at one of the oldest buildings in France. We crossed the bridge over the River Le Clain into the newer part of Poitiers. It was a long, straight walk up a busy commercial street for several kilometers. Following the directions we received at the hotel, we turned left at the University campus and spied the large Super Sports store, which stayed open until well past 6:00 pm, the time we arrived there. They had a good selection of bikes and we picked out two new ones with 18 gears. One was a woman's bike with a luggage rack in place. We had to wait while they put a luggage rack on the men's bike. Our salesman was very helpful and we asked him if they could drive us and our bikes back to our hotel. He said he would ask his superior. When the additions were complete, he said he was sorry, but he couldn't leave the store. He felt bad about not giving us a ride so he decided not to charge us for the extra luggage rack.

It was starting to get dark and we retraced our route, this time on bicycles, back to the hotel. It was so nice to be back on bikes again that we decided not to go straight back. Instead we rode around the city center of Poitiers and then to the south so that we could ride through the Parc de Blossac. This was a small park overlooking the river where strollers enjoyed the evening. By the time we returned to the hotel it was very dark. Our clerk put our bikes into a closet in the parking garage and we went out into the city for a long awaited evening meal.

The next morning we woke up early with the anticipation of starting our journey. We packed our panniers on our bikes, made sure that everything was well positioned, rode out of the parking garage past the front of Hotel Ibis, and down the narrow streets. It was so narrow that we elected to walk on the sidewalks because there was no room for us and the large buses that were traveling the same direction. We rode back into the Parc de Blossac, however, this time we had to walk our bikes down a stairway to the boulevard along the river. We then crossed the River Le Clain and planned on going straight to the west. We rode over the railroad tracks to the south of the station and through a small industrial area before going into the French countryside. We rode into the Foret de Vouille-St-Hilaire, a forest which was very flat and quiet. This gave us a nice hour of pleasant riding toward the village of Benassay. After a short rest on an old stone wall overlooking a riverbank, we meandered through the French countryside for the rest of the morning, trying to follow the route that we had set for ourselves. Whatever we did, we ended up getting back to busy national route, highway N-11. We finally gave up trying to ride on the smaller country roads and just stayed on N-11 until we got to St. Maixent-l'Ecole. In town, we found one of the delightful bakeries, or patisserie, that are so common throughout France. It was filled with a multitude of French pastries, each one more tempting than the one next to it! But first we had a ham and cheese baguette. Then we decided that the pastries could not be passed up and sampled the chocolate éclairs, which hit the spot. We went back for more and tried the coconut macaroons suggested by our server. We walked a while in the town along the main street, poking in and out of the shops for a short time until we decided it was time to get back on our bikes. No matter how hard we tried to fine a quiet road paralleling Highway N-11, we kept coming back to it.

We arrived in Niort in the early evening. We rode south past the industrial complexes to the center of the town. We circled the Place de la Breche, the traditional town square, and found the Hotel Grand on Avenue de Paris. After stowing our bikes in the garage and changing our clothes, we walked across the square to the Rue Victor Hugo, which is a pedestrian shopping street. On the entrance to the street were the Niort dragons. These bronze dragons are 200 meters long and line both sides of the walking street. They commemorate the battle between the beasts and a soldier, Jacques Allonneau, according to a 17ᵗʰ century legend. We followed the street past the market halls, a cathedral of cast iron, glass & metal where local producers and tradesmen sell their wares daily. Next to that stood the Donjon, the town's best known attraction. It is the largest dungeon built exclusively to house prisoners. This large, imposing structure on the River Sevres was built by Henry II in the 12ᵗʰ century. It was later an important prison in the Hundred Years War with England. We crossed the Pont des Arts *(the bridge of arts)* to the Cultural Action Center. This center houses two theaters and several art galleries. More importantly for us, we found a nice restaurant outside the theater with outdoor tables along the river — a most comfortable place to unwind after our day's journey!

ALONG THE RIVER
SEVRES

While unpacking our panniers the night before in our room, I noticed on the town map that there was an area along the River Sevres called La Coulee Verte (*"the green corridor."*) On our way out to dinner that evening, I asked the young man at the hotel desk if it was possible to bicycle along that greenway. He said it was. They were clearing out the river and making the grass acceptable for bicycling. He showed me on a map that you could ride from Niort to the town of Coulon. Another woman at the desk came forward and said you could ride on the greenway, but you could only go up to the highway and then the greenway ends. It became somewhat of a debate at the hotel desk and I was intrigued because the young man assured me it was possible to ride all the way to Coulon. We decided to take that route the next morning.

We thus changed our original plans and instead of going straight south from Niort to Saintes, we decided to try to follow the greenway to Coulon. Coulon is located in the Marais Poitevin, or the marshes of the Poitou area. The marshes have been slowly drained for a thousand years. The area is now a national park. The Venise Verte *("green Venice")* is a wet marsh crisscrossed by canals with heavy vegetation and like marshy areas everywhere, it supports a great abundance of wildlife and birds. The Maraichins who live in this area travel in flat-bottom boats known as *platies*. Boats, such as canoes and paddleboats, can be rented at several areas in the Marais Poitevin. You can also hire your own guides to take you through the marsh.

The next morning we started out on our bikes to see if we could ride to Coulon along the greenway. We left the city of Niort riding past the Plantagenet Donjon on the Sevres River. We crossed the river on Pont des Artes, a small pedestrian bridge to the cultural center where we had eaten the night before. We started riding along the north side of the Sevres River on the Coulee Verte. First, we rode on Quai Maurice Metayer behind some nice houses with pleasant gardens on our right. There were huge rosebushes in full bloom. Houses close to the road had open windows with French blue shutters and flower boxes growing geraniums. We continued on this almost alley-like road for several blocks until the river took a turn. At this point, the river was very picturesque with patches of water lilies in the middle of the river. There were new and some rather old colorful rowboats beached on the side of the river. Within another quarter mile, the road turned into a small park. Families parked in the lot along the river and set up their fishing poles. The poles were extremely long and reached out about 1/3 of the way across the river. They were supported by weights to keep them upright. They were used to fish for the *silure* or sheathfish, the largest and ugliest freshwater fish in France. The park setting only lasted a quarter of a mile and we were soon on a paved bicycle/jogging path, and I thought that this was going to be great — we were on a small, exclusive path along the river. This should be terrific biking!

Shortly thereafter, we crossed under a highway bridge and our paved road came to an abrupt end. Looking ahead, there was a path in front of us with wild vegetation and weeds growing up on both sides. We decided to follow this path for a while and see if it continued in a manner acceptable for biking. We knew we couldn't get lost as long as we stayed along the river, because the river does lead to Coulon. But a distance of 10 km on a dirt path would be difficult biking. Our sense of adventure got the best of us and we started on the path and kept riding. At times the path narrowed down to a width no wider than our bicycle tires. At times the weeds were crushed down and we couldn't see a path at all but we never wanted to turn back. We did manage to follow the river and came to a residential area located on the other side of the river with houses backing to the river.. In a half mile or so we came to a couple picnicking along the river and we asked them if it was possible to ride to Coulon on this path. They said, "Yes, just keep following the path and you will get there." By this point, we were too far to turn back anyway, so we kept riding on the dirt path along the bends in the river where we knew we wouldn't get into too difficult a terrain. The area was beautiful! We heard the constant croaking of bullfrogs along the riverbank and we could see herons standing in the shallows of the river. As we approached them, they would take off to other fishing areas.

Along the River Sevres

After about a half-hour of cycling on this terrain, we noticed a bridge crossing the river to an island. Across the river was a small restaurant called the *Oruisville*

Auberge. Sitting on this island in the Sevres River was the quaintest café imaginable! It was built of stones with woodwork painted in French blue and had awnings to protect the outside tables as well as umbrellas on the patio. Although we had only biked an hour or so that day, we felt we just had to stop at this idyllic setting. Just to sit there and drink coffee along the river was worth the bumps we had experienced the last hour!

Leaving the auberge, we were back on our dirt path which wasn't quite as narrow as it had been before but it was still quite bumpy. As we approached a stand of cottonwood trees, it looked like we were bicycling onto a snow-covered walkway because the cottonwood seeds were thick enough to cover the path for several hundred yards. We continued on this narrow, bumpy path and started to get into a series of gates — every few hundred yards or so somebody had a gated area so we had to get off of our bikes, open up the gate, and walk through, sometimes on wooden boards over little gullies, then close up the gate behind us and ride on to the next gate.

Nearing the town of Magne after one and a half hours, we saw a path that went back to the paved road. We decided to go back up to the road and get off the dirt path. A couple of hundred yards on this road led us right back to the river and a hard dirt path to Coulon. We stopped in the city of Magne for a few minutes and looked at the drawbridge use to cross the river in that area. It looked as if it served its purpose well for many years. The path to Coulon was wider and smoother so we decided to go back to our original plan of riding along the river.. We continued, putting up with the bumpy path and the thick weeds on the edge. We stopped for awhile on the roadside to eat the bananas we had brought from our breakfast that morning. About one half-hour more took us to the town of Coulon. We came off the dirt path, crossed highway D1 and rode down into the village along the river. There were dozens of boats parked alongside the river and restaurants with awnings right on the riverfront. We decided we deserved to sit down for a nice lunch, even though we had only traveled about 8 miles so far that day. We put our bikes up against a fence and sat down at La Pigouille Auberge on the pavement terrace. Being in a marsh, we were tempted to try a local delicacy of eels and butter beans from a clay pot. However, we felt safer having a chevre salad and omelet. We realized we had a lot of time to make up that day, but we did enjoy seeing that it is possible to ride from Niort to Coulon on the Coulee Verte.

Our leisurely lunch was over and we had to "pay the piper" for the time we lost that morning. We left the café at about 2PM and rode past the riverside shops and cafés. We crossed the Sevres river and headed straight south along the D-1 road. The landscape was very rural, so there were no great temptations to stop along the way. We were on a mission to make up for the lost time so we were pedaling hard! We rode through the towns of Epannes and Usseau and eventually turned almost due east when he reached Priaires on the tiny country D-209 road. About 6:00 pm, we reached the town of Surgeres and felt this would be a good place to spend the evening. There were no towns of any size between there and Rochefort and we thought we would have a good chance of finding lodging here. That evening, there was a town-wide sidewalk sale lining the streets as we rode into the town along the Avenue de General De Gaulle. There were items of every kind from used clothes to stacks of old LPs. Farmers had their produce displayed along the street side and there were tables of crafts and local products; it was like all the people of the town cleaned out their garages and basements and stacked it up along the main street. We rode on into the town and found the name of a couple of hotels. The first one was closed so we retraced our route and stopped at the Hotel Gambetta. The hotel was nothing to get excited about – a three-story, stucco, yellowed building on a rather nondescript street with a factory across the way. We were hopeful we could stay here because we really didn't see any other hotel opportunities on our search. We went into the hotel and a pleasant gentleman greeted us. They were busily setting the tables for their evening meal in the dining room. I asked if he had any rooms available and he informed us that they were full. We asked if he could recommend any other hotels nearby and informed him that we were traveling on bicycles and could not go too far to look for another hotel. At that point, he said that he did have a room available on the third floor, but it wasn't made up at this time. If we wouldn't mind waiting for them to prepare the room, we could have that one. I told him there would be no problem with that. We walked around the back and he showed us where to store our bikes for the night. The room located on the third floor was very adequate. It was comfortable and clean and the bathroom was two steps out the door — a good place to spend the night. After cleaning up, we walked around the town that evening. We walked through the continuing street sale toward the castle a few hundred meters from the city center. It was called the Castle of Pere and was built in 1750. We climbed the ramparts and behind the walls was a very beautiful, formal garden and large city park. The castle is best known for its one remaining wrought iron gate with an intricate design. We walked across the park and found an Italian café, Café Roma, across Avenue Saint-Pierre. We had a comfortable dinner of wine and pasta. It was a good way to end a long but challenging day.

SURGERES TO THE COAST

We were up bright and early and ready to leave Surgeres by 8:00 AM. We still had distance to make up from our route change the day before and we were headed to an area that we hadn't originally planned to visit. We would, however, find out that this was an exciting change because of the places the new route would take us. We got our bikes out of the shed in the back of Hotel Gambetta and rode to the center of town. The street sale that was going on the day before was up and rolling again in the morning. We walked down a pedestrian street lined with wares for sale. We realized no matter how much we liked something we found, such as the pieces of brassware and china, we wouldn't be able to take anything with us on our bikes. Further down the walking street was a miniature carousel just the right size for the children to ride on. It seemed to be running on batteries alone and was the kind of thing that got people to visit this small town sale.

At the end of the street, we crossed into the fort that contained the beautiful Church of Notre Dame. We went through the ornate iron gate and rode the length of the park until we exited the south end and got onto Highway 911. It was a fairly busy street leaving the city center. After a couple of miles we exited onto a very quiet country road, D-111, through farmlands traveling almost due west. The rest of the morning was spent in quiet riding.. We rode on small farm roads through several towns. We made one error missing the road we needed to head south. But just beyond we hit the busy highway D-5 and we realized we had gone too far. We circled back and at the town of Cire we found our route and headed straight south toward Rochefort. The roads along the outskirts of Rochefort were lined with poppies in an almost iridescent, orange/red color. We reached Rochefort around 12:30 PM. Rochefort was a very important naval town during the reign of Louis XIV. In 1666, he constructed a city on the River Charente suitable to the tastes of naval officers and travelers. We entered the town through an industrial area surrounded by large piles of scrap iron and imposing factories. As we neared the center of the town, the streets became lined with parks and mansions. We followed directions toward the Place Colbert and found an open square surrounded by shops. Within the square were several outdoor restaurants. We parked our bikes and grabbed a table. We were intrigued while looking at the bill of fare that there were several choices of huitre; you could get an order of 6, 12 or 24 for various prices. When we asked our waiter what huitre was he had a hard time translating it in English. It turns out that there are a great many oyster bays around the area and oysters are very popular at that restaurant. We went ahead and ordered our usual jambon and fromage, ham and cheese, on a baguette along with a small order of huitre. We felt the obligation to sample the local delicacies even if they didn't look too appetizing. Interestingly, in contrast to the tiny carousel we saw earlier that day, the Place Colbert had a very large, ornate carousel sitting in the center of the square. It was a good break for lunch in a very friendly café.

After lunch, we rode down toward the River Charente. We stopped at one of the ubiquitous flower shops and looked at the wares knowing full well we couldn't take any with us. We rode through le Jardin de la Marine and came down to the river at the Corderie Royale or royal ropeworks. Rochefort was the greatest shipyard in 17th century France. It produced 300 vessels per year for Louis XIV in his effort to build up the French navy. He built the Corderie Royale to supply his navy with the ropes for the masts and moorings. In this long, two-story, beautifully restored building, ropes were produced for the French navy for over two centuries. It now houses a naval museum with splendid models of ships as well as demonstrating the technique of rope-making. After riding around this building in a park-like setting, we headed south along the west bank of the river on the Charente pathway. The bicycle path heads south through a marshland the city maintains in an attempt to preserve the flora of the city.

A few hundred yards along the river is the dry dock where the Hermione, an eighteenth century ship, is being reconstructed by the same methods that were used to build the original ship in 1780. This is the ship that brought LaFayette to Boston to help General Washington in the Revolutionary War. This working display is open daily and one can observe shipbuilding skills as they were done in the 1700s.

As we headed farther south, we started to leave the city behind and enter into a combination of parks and industrial areas. Looking to our rear right, we could see an enormous bridge crossing the river. We felt we were fortunate that the bridge was behind us and we wouldn't have to cross such a massive structure. However, as we followed the river further south, the river made a turn and before we knew it, we were heading back to the bridge — it needed to be crossed to continue our way south. The bridge itself had to be seven stories high and as we made our turn from a small bike path to join the auto traffic crossing it, we realized there was a bicycle path set on the edge of the bridge. It was still a very steep climb with cars zooming past us. Upon reaching the apex of the bridge, we had a terrific view looking back towards Rochefort and we had a very quick and easy descent down the other side. On coming off the bridge, we were on a very busy highway but turned off as quickly as possible heading west, riding through the town of Soubise before turning south through the village of Moeze. We then came to the citadel at Brouage. The actual road we were riding on entered the walled structure of the 17th Century fort. This structure once overlooked a thriving harbor but its wealth declined in the later centuries as the ocean receded from its walls. Today, the ramparts of Cardinal Richelieu's previous fortress are filled with shops and restaurants along the cobblestone streets within the citadel itself. It was getting late in the afternoon when we arrived there and the sky was darkening as the threat of rain was increasing. We did, however, have to stop and go through the china shops and nature stores. Here replicas of the wildlife living in the area were for sale. We did make time to stop and have an ice cream along the stone walkways of the old fort.

On leaving Brouage, we had only 4 kilometers to the town of Marennes. Marennes sits on a long bay containing some of the finest oyster beds in France. It is also the gateway via bridge to the second largest French island, the Ile d'Oleron, a very popular resort covered by dunes on its souther coast. We again were on a different long, high bridge heading west across the bay to a peninsula on the Atlantic Ocean. This time the bridge wasn't quite as high and we were used to riding along these high bridges by now, so it wasn't quite the suspenseful experience as our ride across the Charente.

By now it was getting to be dusk. The skies had given us some rain although not too heavy at any time. We felt it was best to find lodging as soon as possible. When we got to the other side of the bridge, we turned to the north and headed for the town of Ronce-le-Bain. It was only a few kilometers from the main road to the town located on the Strait of Maumusson between the peninsula and the Ile d'Oleron. As we neared the town, the roads got narrower and the woods turned into a series of guesthouses and restaurants until at the end of the road we reached the water at a Coney Island type setting. Evidently, Ronce-le-Bain is a very popular destination point for families and young people. As the rain was becoming steadier, we felt the need to find lodging as soon as possible. We rode through the main street in the village. There were parks, miniature golf courses, arcades, restaurants of dubious quality and loud music coming out of many of the bars. We did not find any hotel to our liking in this area and we continued down the coastal street several blocks to the east and came upon the Grand Hotel. We pulled our bikes under the awning of this stately hotel that had none of the tackiness that we had seen earlier in the town. On questioning if there was space available, we were assured that they did have rooms. The desk clerk walked us up two floors to a room with a balcony overlooking the strait, with a beautiful view of the lights from the Ile d'Oleron to the north. We felt that this room was perfect! We cleaned up after our long day of biking, changed into our dry clothes and walked back into the village. We were very happy to sit at a sidewalk café and have burgers and cokes while we watched the vacationers skateboarding down the middle of the road, doing wheelies on their bicycles, and generally having a good visit to this beach town.

RONCES-LES-BAINS TO THE ROYAN FERRY

We awoke the next morning in our hotel overlooking the Strait of Maumusson and now had a view of the Ile d'Oleron across the water. I guess I should say what was left of the water, because the tide had gone out during the night and where during the evening there was water offshore, there was now an area of mudflats. Through our binoculars, we could watch men in waist-high rubber boots harvesting oysters from their beds in the murky water. There were several groups of these oyster gatherers that looked like families of fathers and children working together. We decided to have room service on the balcony that morning. This was a really unusual treat for us. We had a petit dejeuner with china and silverware instead of our usual baguette outside a bakery in some town square. On checking out from the hotel, the clerk told us about a bike path that went all the way along the coast from Ronces-les-Bains on the Atlantic side of the peninsula and south to Royan.

We packed and left the hotel a little bit after 9:00 AM. It was only about a ½-mile ride through the town to the beginning of the trail. The sign at the beginning of the trail said "Foret Domaniale de la Coubre," or the Coubre Forest. There was also something that said this is a bicycle path. Here was a real pedestrian trail with signs prohibiting motorized vehicles on the trail. We started riding west on the flat, paved surface and passed many joggers going in both directions. It was one of those days where the sun would go behind the clouds, the wind would whip up and the rain would start. You would put on your rain jacket and by the time you zipped it up the rain would stop and it would be too hot for the jacket. We rode along the wooded path for several miles until we hit a turn-off that led to the dunes along the Atlantic Ocean. We followed the sandy path through the dunes to Pointe Espagnole and got our first view of the Atlantic. We didn't plan to go that far east in our original route, but going back a few days, the slight change we made in Niort caused us to head almost straight west and ride through this coastal area. We asked the only person we saw along this path to take our pictures with the Atlantic Ocean and dunes in the background. The rain had stopped by now and the breeze off the ocean was very cool. We were really invigorated as we continued biking. We retraced the sandy path from the ocean and got back on the bike path and headed south through a terrain that was mostly sand dunes and low, scrubby vegetation.

As we headed farther south, the traffic on the bike path was increasing. There were a lot of walkers coming from the south and many bicyclists with signs for Club Med on their bikes. As we came up to a harbor, we learned that we were passing the location of Club Med France in this area of the Coubre Forest.

We continued south along the Atlantic and rode past many small resorts with little guesthouses set in the wooded areas away from the ocean. Before the peninsula ended and turned back toward the east, we rode to the lighthouse that has protected this corner of the coast for sailors for hundreds of years. The path at this point ceased to be a pedestrian only road, but turned into a small highway along the coast with wide, sandy beaches. We felt the need to go down to the water to just make sure we touched the Atlantic Ocean. On the Beach de la Palmyre, the road continued along the coast and now we were riding through small towns that most certainly catered to beachgoers in the hot summer months. We rode through St. Palais-s-Mer with its large mansions along the coast and finally through Pontaillac and into Royan.

Royan is a port city at the mouth of the wide Gironde estuary. At the ferry between Royan and Pointe de Grave, the crossing is very wide and takes over 30 minutes to cross. Pointe de Grave is on the tip of the Medoc peninsula containing the famous vineyards of Bordeaux. Not knowing what time the ferry was leaving, we rode along the coast and got right to the ferry port as quickly as possible. We rode up to the ticket window and asked what time the next boat was leaving. The attendant said we had better get going right away because it was leaving in one minute. We paid our fare and cycled down to the two level ferry with cars parked on the lower level and passengers up above. Fortunately for us, we did make a strategic stop in Pontaillac to pick up sandwiches for lunch that day. We secured our bikes in the lower level and went upstairs. We found seats along the edge of the ferry and watched the town of Royan shrink behind us. Ahead was the lighthouse on the other side of the crossing at Pointe de Grave. It was great to sit down and eat our lunch of baguettes with ham and cheese as we made the crossing. We conversed with a couple behind us whose little dog was sitting on their lap shaking, obviously not a fan of seafaring.

LAGUNEAUSSAN

After crossing the mouth of the Gironde River we headed south towards Bordeaux on a busy Highway N215. The ride was pretty straight and flat as we approached the vineyards of the Medoc region. It was getting late in the afternoon as we approached Lesparre-Medoc around 5:00PM. We decided it would be a good time to look for a place to spend the night since it was the only town in the area big enough to have accommodations. As we came into the town and approached the first turnabout, we could see signs for two hotels. We decided to go directly to one of the hotels from that point. We turned off the highway and rode down a commercial street. It didn't take long to find Hotel Paris just a couple of blocks from the turnabout. Unfortunately, the hotel was closed and shuttered. This was not an unusual occurrence for us.

We decided to just ride around the town and see if we could find anything by chance. We went further into the center of the town, away from the highway, and approached a woman and asked her in our most understandable French if she knew of a hotel in Lesparre. She said there was a hotel, Hotel Tours, but we had to go back to the highway and follow it out the other side of the town. We decided to ride through the town and look for other hotels instead of going directly back to the highway. As we were riding through the narrow, rather empty streets of the town, we came across a bakery, or *boulangerie* was actually open late on a Sunday afternoon. We went inside and ordered a big baguette and a couple of Cokes. We sat outside on a bench and just enjoyed the freshly baked French bread and the cooling drinks. I went back inside and talked to the clerk. Again, I asked if she knew of any hotels in the town. She gave us the same advice as the lady on the street. She said that Hotel Tours was on the other side of the town.. She was actually nice enough to call the hotel to see if they had rooms available, which they did and held for us until 6:30 PM. She then gave us a map. Evidently, the Hotel Tours was in a commercial center behind a refrigeration store next to a giant Le Clerq big box department store.

After finishing our French bread, we got back on our bikes and rode out of the town heading south back on N215. The hotel was only supposed to be 5 or 6 kilometers away, but as we traveled down the busy highway, we never did find the hotel. Actually, we rode past the Le Clerq store but did not see a hotel in that development. We thought it might be a little bit farther down the road so we kept on riding another kilometer or two. When we were just about out of the town, I saw a sign for *chambres d'hote*, or guesthouse. I said, "Maybe that's the sign for the hotel." Karen countered, "The sign is too old and too small and wouldn't be appropriate for the hotel that they described to us". We followed the sign anyway. It said 1 kilometer left. "Let's ride down and see what happens." We crossed the busy road and headed down into a wooded area. After riding a few minutes, a rather inebriated looking man passed us on a bicycle and we asked him if he knew of any Bed & Breakfasts down the road. He said there was (as well as he could understand us) and pointed down the road.

We continued on our way and after a few hundred feet more, found the entrance to the guesthouse. As we turned onto the gravel road, we were surprised to see before us a large, beautiful chateau. We rode up the driveway to the front door. The chateau was two stories with extended wings on each side. There was a swimming pool to the side of the house and there was a more formal driveway coming up from our right to the center of the house. There were also several small buildings and a barn on the nearby property. By this time, it was just getting dark outside. I knocked on the door and waited for an answer. Eventually, a man in his early 40s came to the door. I first asked him, "Parlez-vous Anglais?" He said, "Oui, I am from Holland and we all speak English." I said, "Good, that makes it easier for us to talk. Do you have a room available for the night?" He said, "Yes, we do. You are welcome to stay here. We weren't planning a formal dinner for tonight, but you are welcome to stay and have dinner with us. We will just be having pizza but I think you will find it enjoyable." "That sounds good for us!" I answered. He directed us to take the packs off our bikes, set them down by the front door, and to bring the bikes around to one of the garages in the back. He brought us into the house and up the stairs to our room over the front door. The room was quite large with a high ceiling and several beds. We had a view of the front yard from out window. It was obviously remodeled quite recently because the bathroom was very up-to-date. We told him that the room would be just fine. He suggested that we get comfortable and that dinner would be at 7:30 in the kitchen. We were to make ourselves at home, feel free to walk around the grounds, or explore the main floor of the house.

After unpacking our bags, taking a shower and getting out of our biking clothes, I went downstairs. I noticed the photographs on the wall of a home in Holland. There was also an interesting piece of equipment that I later found out was an iron to press clothes. It was about the size of a coffee table and was also brought with other furniture from Holland. I went down to the kitchen to talk to the Dutchman, whose name was Laban. He and his brother had just purchased the chateau within the last year and were in the process of converting it into a

Bed & Breakfast. He told me that the chateau used to be a vineyard, but there had been no grapes grown there for the last 20 years. It was called *Chateau Laguneaussan,* which means "lagoon filled in with sand" (or silt). They were thinking about restarting the vineyard, but that was a plan for the future. He was a retired architect and this was his next phase of life.

About this time, his friend, Pim, came in. Pim does most of the maintainence around the chateau. They had grown up together in Zeeland, the Dutch province made up of a series of islands in the southern part of the country. They adopted two dogs that were living with them and kept them chained up in the house. The dogs seem very content to remain chained under the stairs. I asked if I could take the dogs out for a walk and they said that I could. So before dinner that night, I went for a walk with the dogs, Joop and Bobo. We walked on part of the 150 acres to the wooded areas out by the formal driveway. There was a massive, impressive Cedar of Lebanon tree right in front of their driveway that must have been there for 400 years. There were donkeys in the front pasture. I walked around to the side past the swimming pool. The dogs seemed to be leading me on the best places to walk on their property!

I came back into the house, chained the dogs up, and they quietly laid down. By this time, Karen had finished showering and was downstairs. A big fire had been built in the kitchen fireplace, which felt good because it was getting cool at sunset. We sat around the large, wooden Dutch table in the kitchen and they served champagne before dinner. At this time, Laban's brother, Hans, came in. Hans does most of the farming and takes care of the land. He had been out in the woods clearing out the brush from the roadside. We were then served strawberries with cream along with our champagne. After a couple of glasses of champagne, the conversation came easily and we talked about the recent referendum where the French turned down the constitution for the European union. I heard their opinion from a Dutch point of view about what they felt was important. We talked about our experiences biking through Zeeland 25 years ago, and heard about their travels through Europe and to the US. Dinner flowed on very comfortably. About this time the pizza was ready and Hans, who was in charge of the pizza, pulled it out of the oven and served it up. It tasted very good with the local Medoc wine. A salad was served in the customary French manner after the entrée. We heard the stories of how they found their two dogs, how they kept property that they owned in Amsterdam, and rented out houses. After several glasses of wine, we were quite relaxed! Dessert was a Greek yogurt with honey, which hit the spot at the end of a long day.

After dinner, we walked around the first floor of the house which was decorated with furniture that they brought from Holland. Laban settled down in front of the TV set in the living room and we went upstairs to our room and "crashed" after a day that included 10 hours of biking.

The next morning, we awoke early after a good night's sleep. We packed our bags and as is our habit, got our biking clothes out for the day. I went downstairs early and went for a walk with the dogs. This time, I went out the back into the wooded area and walked to the fence line. We couldn't eat breakfast until 8:30 because that was the time the fresh bread was delivered. Breakfast was typically what we received in France and consisted of several types of breads, baguettes, croissants, and even a chocolate croissant. We had café au lait, a strong coffee with an abundance of hot milk poured in it. Pim was going to work on fixing their tractor that day. Hans was going out to work on the fence where the donkeys were kept. Laban seemed to be hanging around the house more than the others.

After packing our panniers onto our bikes, we asked all of them to come out so we could take a picture of them in front of the chateau. We all lined up underneath the Cedar of Lebanon tree and took several pictures. We were very fortunate to find such a charming place to spend the night when, as of 6:00 the night before, we had no place to stay. It was also good that they spoke English so we could have a really nice conversation during dinnertime. We bid our hosts adieu and we were directed to head out the back of the property, which would put us on the road to the Medoc wineries. As we rode out, Hans followed us with a bicycle — I'm not sure if he was there to say goodbye or to make sure we locked the back gate, but we said goodbye and headed to the south from the *Chateau Laguneaussan.*

CHATEAU
BRANAIRE-DUCRU

We left the back gate of the Chateau Laguneaussan and headed out onto a quiet highway, D204. There was very little traffic during this morning hour and we soon started seeing the vineyards of the famous Bordeaux area appearing on both sides of the road. Little by little as we traveled south, we could see more vines covering the hillsides. Soon we came to view some of the fabulous chateaus associated with each of the vineyards. A chateau includes the vineyard and a building, which can range from the most modest to the most elegant. Their philosophy was to have a building associated with the land where the grapes were grown. This gave the buyers of the wine the feeling that there was great stability of each particular vineyard. In many cases, the chateaus were spectacular palaces. We headed south on D204 through different appellations or wine-growing districts. If you have ever read the label of a bottle of Bordeaux wine, you can easily identify which appellation the wine came from.

We rode through Saint-Estephe and then into Pauillac. In the Pauillac appellation, we came across one of the most spectacular chateaus and one of the most well known Bordeaux wines, Chateau Mouton Rothschild. We pulled off the side of the road and peered through the large iron gate surrounding the chateau and saw gardens between the building and the impressive facade. As we were standing there, a large van pulled up next to us and asked us if we knew what chateau that was. I told the driver that I thought it was Mouton Rothschild. He got out of his van and we started talking. He had driven his van from Austria and was interested in touring the chateaus. His wife then got out with their little poodle, Stephanie, and suggested we try to get on one of the tours of the chateau. We followed them up the road off the highway into the vineyards. I knew you needed to make reservations to visit the chateaus well in advance, particularly the most famous ones. Before we left, our friends at Chateau Laguneaussan told us to go to Chateau Branaire-Ducru and they would be able to take us on a tour without booking reservations at the tourist office. Anyhow, we tried with our Austrian acquaintances but we found out the tours that day were booked solid and most were conducted in French. We did take our time and walked around to the front of the chateau overlooking the man-made lakes. There were rather extensive formal gardens, which in itself would have been a nice place to visit. Upon realizing that we were not going to see anymore at Chateau Mouton-Rothschild, we bid adieu to our Austrian friends and headed back on our bikes continuing south on the road.

Cycling past the vineyard Chateau Pichon Longueville

We passed another of the famous chateaus, Château Lafite Rothschild, among many smaller chateaus. Lafite Rothschild and Mouton Rothschild are two of the most highly rated Bordeaux wines. In 1855, Napoleon III asked the organization of the Bordeaux wine growers to arrange their wines into classifications according to quality. This is known as the 1855 Crus Classifications. Those chateaus are two of only five wines that have the premiere Crus class, making them the highest quality of Bordeaux wines available. The Bordeaux wines are further broken down into the Grand classes, of which there are approximately 60, then into lesser classifications such as the 400 Crus Bourgeois and 300 Crus Artisans.

We rode out of the appellation Pauillac and into the appellation of Saint-Julien Beychevelle. It was in this appellation that the chateau we were looking for, Branaire-Ducru, was located. On finding its sign along the road we turned into their vineyard. At first we couldn't see the chateau, but we could see the large vineyards growing along the roadside. As we turned into the group of small buildings, we could then see the chateau of the Branaire-Ducru vineyards. It wasn't the palatial façade of Chateau Mouton Rothschild, but it was a very attractive two-story manor. We turned into a parking lot, got off our bikes and walked over to a building labeled "Office." We went into the business office and asked the young ladies at the desk if we could tour the property. At first, the woman in charge at the desk said that it wouldn't be possible because it was right during their lunchtime. I wasn't about to take "no" for an answer this easily and explained to her that the Dutchmen at Chateau Laguneaussan told us that they were very cordial at this chateau and would be willing to give us a tour because of their friendship. I also told the young woman, whose name we later found out was Yvonne, that my wife would be very disappointed if we weren't able to take a tour. She looked at the clock and said, "Well, I guess we could take you on a tour."

First, she walked us out into the vineyards near the office and showed us the growth of the small vines. She explained how they tended each of the vines and made sure they were growing healthy without any type of disease. Then we turned back and she was going to take us to the vat house. Outside the office was a young couple talking to the president of the chateau, Patrick Maroteaux, and she introduced us and he asked if the Ukrainian couple could accompany us on our tour. We soon had the four of us on the tour and were shortly joined by an American couple who raced to catch us before we entered the vat house. Although wine has been grown on this property since the 17th Century and the chateau itself was built in 1824, the vat house was built in 1988 and was very modern with large, stainless steel vats and a progressive gravity flow system, which eliminates the need to pump the harvest and wine. This allows the grapes to keep the natural expression of the Branaire-Ducru "terroir". This is the belief that a wine's character is due to the quality of the land. The vat house contained hundreds of large, oak barrels to age the wines. The wine remains in those barrels for 16-22 months before they are bottled.

Next came the best part of the tour, the wine tasting—we tasted a bottle of 2004. Then we were given a taste of a 2003, which was even smoother and more pleasant than the 2004 wine. This was quite a treat. Chateau Branaire-Ducru is a fourth Crus in the 1855 classification, which rates it approximately as one of the top 50 Bordeaux wines. After finishing the tour of the vat house, we walked back to the office and thanked Yvonne. We asked her if she would mind if we ate our lunch, salami and cheese sandwiches that we had purchased earlier in the day, at the little gazebo to the side of the chateau. She said that would be fine. We grabbed our sandwiches and our bottles of water and walked over to the seats in the gazebo and enjoyed our lunch while looking out over the vineyards.

After a few minutes, Mr. Maroteaux came out of his office in the chateau with a bottle of 2004 Bordeaux and said, "I think your lunch would be much more enjoyable with a bottle of wine rather than bottles of water." He then opened up the bottle for us and poured the wine into the glasses that he had also brought out with him and sat with us for a few minutes. He told us that he was in our hometown of St. Louis on a selling trip just a few years earlier. He also told us that he had been chairman of the chateau since 1988 and it had always been a goal of his to direct a chateau. He had his digital camera with him and took our picture enjoying his wine in the gazebo and told us he would e-mail the pictures to us. He was most gracious to greet us with such fine hospitality. It made our visit to Chateau Branaire-Ducru a real highlight of our ride through the Bordeaux region.

ARRIVING
IN BORDEAUX

We left the Chateau Branaire-Ducru winery in good spirits. We were well nourished. Sharing a fine bottle of red wine with lunch completed the visit. We were very careful as we got back on the highway since we are not accustomed to bicycling after drinking alcoholic. However, that did not affect our riding. We continued south on the sparsely traveled D-2 highway and about ten kilometers down the road, we got a view of the beautiful Margaux chateau. Built in 1802, its Palladian façade is home to one of the five first Crus of the Bordeaux classifications, one of the top five rated Bordeaux wines. As in the case of the most popular vineyards, the tours of the facility are sold out in advance and we were not able to tour the Margaux vineyards. No matter how good their wines, I am sure their hospitality couldn't match that which we had just received at Branaire-Ducru.

We rode on and had some beautiful views of the Gironde River. Just north of Bordeaux the Gironde splits into the Garonne, which goes straight south to Bordeaux and the Dordogne, which heads to the east. We followed the road and soon saw the sign at the border, "Entering Bordeaux". Bordeaux is the biggest city we rode through on our entire trip. As we crossed under the northern circumferential highway we rode into an area called Le Lac. It contains a large lake surrounded by beaches and jogging trails. We took advantage of the trails by using on them to get out of the traffic. We watched windsurfers out on the lake. We realized that it would take some good navigating to get to our hotel.

As we went past the lake, we turned south again onto a very busy, urban street. As we were waiting at a light, a man on a bicycle pulled up next to us and we asked him in our best French how to get to the city center. He was very accommodating and motioned for us to follow him. For the next couple of miles, we rode behind him without talking at all. When he turned off the street, he pointed the direction that we should take.

Bordeaux is a large city of 300,000 people. The busy streets were very beautiful. They were lined with trees in front of the five-story residential buildings through the northern part of town. When we saw the

River Garrone, we knew that if we rode along the river we would definitely get ourselves to the city center. So we rode along the river until we saw the park-like Esplanade de Quinconces. This vast square was laid out in 1820 to commemorate the twenty-two National Assembly deputies executed here during the French Revolution. Our hotel was located on a pedestrian street, rue St. Catherine. As we rode away from the river, we passed the Grand Theatre, a fine, 18th century, neoclassical building. The auditorium is known for its fine acoustics and spectacular staircase later imitated by Garnier at the Paris Opera. We then walked our bikes through the busy pedestrian streets adjoining the newly constructed trolley system. After walking along rue St. Catherine, we saw our hotel. There was a very small lobby off the corner of the street. Unfortunately, most of the hotel was built over a busy McDonald's restaurant. We locked our bikes outside and went in to register. We asked the front desk clerks if he knew anyone who might be interested in buying our bikes. I don't think they ever took us seriously because they never really gave us an answer. I think they thought we were just joking. We did find a place in the hotel to keep our bikes overnight and we brought them into the narrow hallway and then carried them down a steep flight of stairs to the cellar and left them amongst the hotel's supplies.

The Grand Theatre of Bordeaux

That evening, we enjoyed walking through the pedestrian streets around our hotel. We stopped in an athletic shop called "Sports Line" on rue St. Catherine and hoped that we could sell our bikes that evening. They said that they were not able to purchase bikes. We then wandered down the rue de la Porte Dijeaux and through the old gate into the Place Gambetta, a park in the middle of an old part of the city. We enjoyed our dinner sitting at a streetside café called the Pub au Bureau. One of their specialties is flammekueche. This is an Alsatian dish composed of thin bread dough covered with crème fraiche, or fresh cream, and quark, a soft central European white cheese, sprinkled with onions and bacon. It is cooked very quickly over an intense fire. I thought of it as a wonderful white cheese pizza. With a bottle of Stella Artois it was a delightful place to end our evening.

The next morning we went in earnest to try to sell our bicycles. After again being snubbed at our hotel desk, we wandered over to the Office of Tourism. They were quite helpful and told us about a shop where they loan bikes to students in Bordeaux. We thought that would be a very sensible place to look since they would need to have bikes to loan out. So we rode south through the city to the shop. We stood in line with several students waiting for the shop to open and asked them about the availability of the bikes there. They told us that with a small deposit, they could get a loaner bike for the time they are studying in Bordeaux. It was a very inexpensive way for them to have transportation. When the office opened we were soon able to talk to one of the clerks. They said that they were not in a position to buy any bikes That is done through a different organization but he directed us to a bike shop that might be interested.

We rode farther south in the city to the rue Cour l'Ysur and came to the station Velo Services. We found the shop full of new and used bikes and the proprietor was very busy taking care of repairs and sales on his own. He said he would be interested in buying our bikes and we made a successful transaction, although we received less than we were hoping for in the sale. However, he told us that on our return for the next leg of our trip, if we were to e-mail him several weeks in advance, he would have bikes prepared for us. So, although it wasn't the ideal way to dispose of our bikes, it was a very fortunate finding. And who knows? When we begin the fourth leg of our trip, we might be all set to go without having to search the city for bicycles.

Leg Four:
Bordeaux to Spain

May, 2007

RETURN TO BORDEAUX

We arrived in Bordeaux on the Trains a Grande Vitesse, or TGV, right on schedule. That in itself was an achievement, since all night the monitors on the airplane had us arriving 45 minutes late. The plane sat on the runway at JFK for about 45 minutes before taking off. We had just under an hour and a half to disembark the plane, retrieve our baggage, go through customs, mail our boxed suitcase to St. Jean de Luz and make it to the railroad station, fortunately, located within Charles de Gaulle airport. When we arrived a few minutes early, we were overjoyed that we would be able to make the 8:55 train as planned. We got our checked bag, which was only the one suitcase already boxed up for the post office, and got through customs with no delays. We decided to carry on our panniers and everything we needed to start our biking trip in case our luggage didn't make it on time. With our boxed suitcase in tow, we headed to the post office with plenty of time. Unfortunately, the post office didn't open until 8:30 AM and we arrived there a few minutes before

8:00. There still was plenty of time to make our train. We were the first to queue up at the door and found comfortable positions sitting on the floor outside the post office. We made sure we would be the first ones served at the desk.

The fact that the train station was a few minutes walk was quite comforting. However, 8:30 AM came and went and the doors did not open. By 8:40, we felt that we couldn't wait any longer and quickly headed to the airport train station, pushing our cart with our panniers and suitcase. We arrived at the platform with only minutes to spare, found our compartment and stowed our luggage in the racks at the end of the car.

The TVG are high speed trains that can go from Paris to Bordeaux in a little over three hours. Even traveling at speeds up to 180 MPH, they are very comfortable to ride in. We had a small compartment with four seats and a table in the middle. Fortunately, there was no one sitting across from us, so we could lean back and put our feet up on the chairs across from us. We leaned our heads back against the pillows, looked out at the landscape and saw the countryside in a blur as we sped by. We could recognize places we had previously biked as we crossed the Loire River at Tours and we could see the long stairway to the old part of Pointiers that led from the train station. As we left the railroad station in Bordeaux, we were familiar with the recently installed tram system in Bordeaux. We dragged our gear to the tram C stop knowing it would end at the Esplanade des Quinconces, about a half block from our hotel.

What we didn't remember was how to get a ticket to ride the tram. I did obtain cash at the airport before we left that morning, but I didn't have small enough denominations to purchase tickets at the automatic dispenser. I did not see anywhere else where I could get tickets. The first tram C came and went. I then had to go into a bakery at the station and get change for the ticket dispenser. I inserted a euro into the dispenser to buy tickets and found that the coin slot was jammed. I wasn't about to put bills in this questionable machine again and we missed the second tram that pulled out. I then tried to buy tickets in the tabac (the smoke shop), which did sell tickets for the tram. Unfortunately, they only sold tickets in booklets of ten. An Englishman buying tickets at the same time said he would be glad to sell me two tickets from his ten, but on trying to accomplish that, we realized he didn't actually get individual tickets, but a pass for the ten rides. Finally, we went back and got on a tram without a ticket and "stole" a ride to the center of Bordeaux.

It is a short tram ride from the Gar St. Jean and at the end of the 15-minute trip we got off at the terminal next to the Esplanade des Quinconces in the center of Bordeaux. We walked past the vendors selling ice cream and balloons in this popular park. We then went about half a block down the narrow street rue de

Condé to the Hotel Majestic. Here we were welcomed by the desk clerk Mademoiselle Renee. Since our room was not ready, she told us to store our belongings behind the desk. We still had our suitcase with us, so we asked directions to the nearest post office and carried the box out of the hotel. Our street ended right at the Grand Theatre, the Bordeaux landmark from the days of the Second Empire. The stone statues of the nine muses along the columned arcade might have enjoyed seeing us transport our suitcase down the street.

We passed the travel offices where people were lining up their tours of the Bordeaux vineyards and headed down the boulevard Allees de Tourny for about a block to the post office . Again, we were unlucky as the post office door was locked. We knocked with no result. The workmen at the next shop walked over and pointed to the hours on the door, *"Closed from 12:00-14:00"*. Fortunately, it was only about 15 minutes until it opened, so we crossed the street and sat in the park on the boulevard and waited. A few minutes later a clerk returned from lunch. When our turn came up, we successfully sent our suitcase via the French postal service to St. Jean de Luz, the final stop of our trip south. We were a little concerned when the clerk couldn't find the name of our town and asked if it was located in France. Anyhow, it was on its way and we were free from having to lug it any more, at least for a while!

Our next and most important task before we could begin was to get our bikes. We decided to rent the bikes this year. In corresponding with Emmanuel at the Station Velo Services in the preceding months, he suggested renting the bikes for 59 euros. In the past, we had bought and sold our bikes, but seeing as our train from the south had to pass through Bordeaux on the way back, we decided to go ahead and rent the bikes this trip. We walked past the opera house and down the long pedestrian street, St. Catherine. We window shopped and crossed the rue Victor Hugo. The complexion of the street changed at that point to lower class vintage clothing and tattoo shops. We reached the place de Victoire located in a university setting. A few blocks left on the cours de la Marne, we found cours de l'Yser, where the shop was located. It looked familiar from our previous visit there and we turned to the right. "Please still be there," I muttered to myself as we walked down the street.

The shop was a little farther down than I remembered, but eventually we did come across the Station Velo Services bike shop. The door to the front was open and as we went in, we were met by a young man. I asked, "Are you Emmanuel? We are here to pick up a rental." "No, I am Victor, but I do know about the bikes you are supposed to rent." He pulled out two decent appearing bikes, not new by any stretch of the imagination, but serviceable. He pumped up the tires, adjusted the seats for us and gave us locks — it seemed that everything was in order. We asked Victor for directions to leave Bordeaux in the direction of the Archachon Basin and he told us the best way to leave the city. We felt like we knew where we were headed the next day. We thanked Victor and brought our bikes for the next week out of the store.

It was fun riding again. Although the streets we rode on were very busy, we soon worked our way to an area with quieter streets that lead to the Garonne riverfront. Since we had been there last, the riverfront had really changed. They had built walkways along a great stretch of the river that were popular with bicyclists, roller bladders and walkers. Along the river were playgrounds and wading pools and further down the river was a new development with shops. We rode all the way past the Esplanade des Quinconces because biking was just so pleasant that afternoon. We stopped at an ice cream shop and treated ourselves to a late afternoon dessert.

We then returned to our hotel via the central gardens in the city. The clerk had brought our bags up to our room and we were directed to the garage where we could keep our bikes for the night. Everything was now in order: we had our bikes for the trip, we had our directions out of the city and we were ready to begin the last leg of our journey across France.

LEAVING BORDEAUX

We arose early and eager to start the last leg of our journey. Glancing out of our hotel window, we could see a light rain moistening the red tiled roofs of Bordeaux. After a *petit dejeuner* in the breakfast room, we went down to the garage to load our packs on the bikes. The first time putting packs on a different bike is always a challenge. You've got to be sure that your panniers are far enough back so the pedals won't hit them. Also, you have to be sure that everything is securely fastened. But doing this for the fourth time, we were pretty proficient at it and were soon ready to ride. We walked our bikes out of the garage onto the rue de Conde. I wouldn't say that it was really raining. Rather it was misting when we started to ride at 9:00 AM. We passed the Grand Theater as we turned off rue de Conde. We rode south on the pedestrian street rue St. Catherine and as we coasted by shopkeepers were washing the streets, unloading their wares, and cleaning their windows before the start of the business day.

Ordinarily, when leaving a large city it is a challenge to head in the right direction without getting on a busy highway. Victor at Station Service Velos gave us good directions. We rode past the Cathedral St. Andre, the finest of Bordeaux's churches. It was consecrated in 1096 at the time of the first Crusade. We stopped to take a quick look inside the cathedral. Just past St. Andre's, we turned left at the city hall and headed south, looking for rue de Pessac. After five or six blocks, we hit rue de Pessac and turned to the west. For the next hour, we rode on busy urban streets. Rue de Pessac was a crowded street lined with shops and offices. We stayed in the bus lane on the right as we left Bordeaux.

We entered the village of Pessac by simply crossing a street from Bordeaux. It was still crowded, but not as congested. Gradually, the traffic lessened and the rue de Pessac turned into N250, a long, straight road with ample traffic. Both sides of the road were covered with forests set about 50 feet back. The forest was a solid growth of pine trees. Between the trees and the road, there was low-growing, scrubby vegetation. After riding a short time, Karen mentioned, "I feel like I'm riding uphill – there must be something wrong with my bike." At that point, we switched bikes and I certainly felt that riding this bike was not as easy to ride as the one I had been on, but it seemed to be okay (more on this later).

At the town of Marcheprime we decided it wouldn't be wise to ride to the Arcachon Basin for lunch. This is a very popular tourist area on a large, inland bay due west of Bordeaux. It would take us slightly out of our was to the north. We decided it would be advantageous to go southwest toward our evening destination, so we turned onto D5 and quickly exited onto D216 at les-Quatre-routes, which we followed for a long way towards Biscarosse. One thing that broke the monotony was the appearance of celebratory living trees in front of houses. These pine trees were covered with various decorations like artificial flowers, colored balls and ribbons. Most of them had a picture of someone and had a quotation about the event. We learned later that in this area, the people decorate these trees only in the month of May to honor people's achievements — things like birthdays, graduations and promotions. They were fun to see and reminded us of Christmas trees in May. We stopped in the small town of Mios for lunch. The café was full of families having their Saturday afternoon meal together.

After a nice lunch and a discussion about traveling in the US with one of the patrons who taught English at the local school, we headed down D652 to Biscarosse. The ride on this road was long, straight and uneventful and riding the poorly performing bike made the long trip even longer! Occasional colorfully decorated May trees perked up the landscape. We passed the small town of Sanguinet in mid afternoon. We looked for a bicycle shop in the town without any luck. We soon reached Biscarosse. Biscarosse is a town located on a lake of the same name. There is a string of lakes just inland from the Atlantic Ocean with Lake Cazaux to the north and Lake Mimizan to the south. The town has an associated beach or *plage* to the west on the Atlantic. We rode into Biscarosse and found a large tourist map on the outskirts of the town. The tourist information center and many of the hotels were located in more touristy Biscarosse Plage, which was another 10 km northwest. Since it was 5:00 PM and would be out of our way the next morning, we elected to stay in Biscarosse Centre-Ville. We also learned looking at the map that there is a series of bike paths throughout the area that make circuits around the lakes.

There were advertisements for a few hotels so we rode around the town center. The center was relatively modern with shops and cafes surrounding a market area. We finally settled on Hotel Atlantide just off the town marketplace. Its brochure pictured it right on the beach but that wasn't the case. It was a pleasant enough hotel. Justine, the clerk, let us put our bikes in the garage behind her apartment for safekeeping that night. We walked around the town and passed the Musse de l'hydraviation, probably the only seaplane museum in the world. In the center we found a nice café serving crepes and wine. After dinner, we walked back to the hotel for a good night's sleep. That evening a heavy thunderstorm shook the windows in our room!

BISCARROSSE
TO THE LANDES

The next morning the rain had stopped. We looked out the window of the Hotel Atlantide and were relieved to see that the heavy, driving rain from the previous night had ended. While having *petit dejeuners* in the breakfast room, the sun started to break through the clouds and actually a nice day was developing. After a hearty breakfast, we retrieved our bikes from the garage in the next building and loaded our gear.

We rode away from the hotel through Place Marsan, where a farmer's market was taking place. There was a bread maker with a large wood-burning oven. Unfortunately, we had just eaten our fill of French bread at breakfast so we couldn't sample any. Another booth was stacked with wheels of fresh cheese and we got a sample of cabecou, a creamy goat cheese. We walked on through the various stalls of fruits and vegetables and CDs and clothes. From there, we headed to the soccer stadium to look for the *piste cyclable,* or bicycle path to head south. *Stade Triscos* was an appropriate size for a small town. I could imagine the spectators urging on their local teams in this setting. On the opposite side was the bike path. After riding past the soccer field, we headed south on an asphalt path between the backyards of small houses.

We could now travel free from traffic and observe the flower and vegetable gardens behind the small homes. Soon the path joined Highway D652 and paralleled the highway on the way to Parentis-en-Born. It was so relaxing being on a separate bicycle path that we just seemed to glide past markets and factories on our way to Parentis. At this time, even the difficulty of pedaling the defective bike was of minimal concern. We saw a direction sign to Mimizan, our next main destination. "There's probably lots of roads to Mimizan," I told Karen. "We have to get to Parentis before turning off." We were hypnotized by the smooth ribbon of asphalt.

About 20 minutes later, we still hadn't reached the town. The path was so nice but I thought maybe I should ride over to the road we were paralleling to see if I could figure out where Parentis was. We cut down a dirt path to the road and found out we were paralleling D43, heading due east. We were going the wrong way. We turned around and retraced our route past the brick factory and the fire station we had just passed. We talked to a fireman or *pompier,* who explained there was a cycle path to Mimizan. We were excited to find it. It actually was where we saw the sign to Mimizan 45 minutes earlier.

We did lose some time but we were cruising on our way until my bike jerked to a dead stop. I skidded to a halt and jumped off before I fell. I could barely get my pedals to turn. Looking at the wheels, I could see that one of the bungee cords was caught in the rear gears. We turned the bike over and untangled the cord. It unraveled very easily. Ordinarily, this would be no problem. However, with the previous difficulty pedaling this proved to be the "straw that broke the camel's back". The bike became almost impossible to ride. I righted the bike and could barely turn the pedals. Every revolution of the pedals caused the rear brakes to constrict. As Karen rode behind me, she said the rear wheel was wobbling back and forth on rotation. So, on a Sunday morning with a defective bike, we had no choice but to push on. We waved down a family biking towards us and asked if there were any bike shops in the area. They didn't know of any and our best bet was in Mimizan.

Soon the bike path ended and we were back on D562 with light, but steady, traffic. A sign said "Mimizan 21 km", so we knew we had a ways to go. The bike was rideable but every rotation of the pedals was like going up a cliff. We anxiously started watching for bicycle shops now. In the town of Gastes, on the south end of Lake Biscarrosse, there wasn't even a store and further in St. Eulalie-en-Born everything was closed. Past there, the road changed to D87 and on our right was a barbed wire fence around a large military zone. To our left we could see the *etang* or Lake D'Aureilhan. It was nice having a lake to watch as we rode. Soon after the lake we got our crippled bike to Mimizan.

Like Biscarrosse, Mimizan has Mimizan Centre and Mimizan Plage, or beach. I thought our best bet to find an open shop was in the touristy Mimizan Plage but seeing as we came to Mimizan Centre first we decided to take a swing around it. We soon came across a huge sporting goods store, "Sport 2000" that sold bikes. We could see that it opened at 8:00 AM on Monday. We decided to keep riding around Mimizan and look for another place. We passed the 13th Century Abbey Church bell tower but didn't have a desire to stop. After an uphill climb, we joined D626 and headed the 8 kilometers west to the plage. We could feel the salt air as we reached the Atlantic. We were soon riding into the entrance to Mimizan Plage. We crossed the last street and entered the pedestrian area. There were restaurants, T-shirt shops and bars on both sides of the walkway — a Coney Island atmosphere. We walked our bikes through the crowded concourse. We were trying to decide what to have for lunch. With all our bicycle tribulations, it got to be almost 2:30 PM before we thought about food.

We went up to one of the food stands and asked if there were any bicycle shops around. We were told there was one on the next street. We hoped it would be open on Sunday. We walked over and found the shop, O$_2$ Cycles, with dozens of rental bikes in front. We went in and talked to the proprietor, who said his name was Norbert. He looked at my bike and said that the wheel was shot. He could fix it in about half an hour. He also said the bike was not adequate to carry so much gear. He asked where we rented our bikes and I explained that we rented them in Bordeaux. He said he worked in Bordeaux and he would take our wheel back and tell the people at Velo Service about our problems and see if they would reimburse us. We left our gear in his shop and walked back to the pedestrian area and ordered a lunch of baguette sandwiches and Cokes. We walked over to the beach, dodging skateboarders as we went. It was refreshing to sit overlooking a large, sandy Atlantic beach and have our lunch. It was also encouraging to know that we could get on with our trip and not have to return to Mimizan Centre tomorrow and wait for my bike to be repaired.

As we walked back to the bike shop, we browsed in the shops. During the busy summer holidays, I bet these places would be packed! When we got back my bike was fixed. We thanked Norbert profusely. I loaded on my gear and we were ready to journey on. It was now about 3:30 PM. With our morning mistaken route and the bike defect we were several hours behind schedule. Norbert gave us directions to the piste cyclable heading south. We rode south through the beach town and crossed a bridge leaving Mimizan . We were looking for the northern end of a bicycle path. I noticed a small red line on a map years ago. The line denoted a bicycle path along the coast. We were soon going to find out what this path was like. We got some help from another cyclist on the road going out of town. Realizing we couldn't speak French, he motioned for us to follow him and we rode hard to keep up. It was great to have the bicycle repaired so pedaling was smooth again. After a few blocks and a few more turns, he pointed in the direction of a path headed into a parking area. We thanked him and rode down the path to the beginning of a piste cyclable de la cote, or cycle path of the coast.

PISTE CYCLABLE DE LA COTE

We entered the *Piste Cyclable de la Cote* just before 4:00 PM. This was our introduction to the Landes region of southwest France. We rode out of the parking area into a dark primeval forest. There were dense stands of pine trees and the terrain was low, rolling hills. At times, the ground was overrun with ferns. The ocean was to our west but rarely in sight. However, we still felt the sensation of the humid salt air as we rode through the forest.

In actuality, this was not a primeval forest in the true sense. The Landes region, literally meaning moors, was a region of marshland. It was so wet that shepherds developed stilts to walk through the bogs when tending their flocks. It was a difficult land to farm and survive in. In the mid 19th Century Napoleon III ordered the planting of maritime pines to stabilize the land. The swamps were drained and protective dunes were built to reclaim the land. Today, the forest encompasses one million hectacres and is Europe's largest cultivated forest.

We rode on a thin ribbon of asphalt in the area called the *foret de Mimazin,* or forest of Mimazin. There are 200 kilometers of *piste cyclable* on the Landes coast. Most were paved by the Germans during WWII. There are also ample hiking trails in the French Grande Randonnees system, the cross-country hiking routes. As we began riding, we encountered a slight shower, just enough that we felt we should put on our rain gear before we got too wet. However, the shower was never more than a drizzle and this was the only time we had to don our rain gear. We encountered very few cyclists but occasionally we would pass a group of hikers. Every few miles we came to a cross-road heading west to the beach. We would see more people in these areas than in the deeper woods. At Contis-Plage, we turned west into the beach town. We circled a small village until we found a good place to stop and sample ice cream from the local vendor. A pause along the coast with an ice cream cone was a nice break!

Bicycle path in the Landes

On leaving town, we couldn't find the way back to the cycle path. Not being sure which trail to take, we rode back into town. We were told to take the road directly in front of us and go over the pink bridge. I was skeptical about finding a pink bridge but we followed the directions. One thing about this area is the numerous camping areas. They are not for tent camping or even RVs, but large collections of permanent cabins and huts that the city dwellers flock to during their vacations. With the proximity to the ocean and forest air, they must be packed in August, the traditional vacation time in France. As we rode along the very quiet D403 road between two large vacation camps, the pink bridge appeared — it was definitely pink! There was no doubt we were headed in the right direction. We turned off the road and got back on the cycle path in the *foret de Lit-et-Mixe* and continued south.

It was getting close to 6:00 PM. The sun didn't set until 9:00, but we didn't want to get caught without a place to stay for the night. We felt the urgency to push on. The maritime pines in the Landes characteristically lose their lower branches, so the lower three-fourths of the trees are almost just tree trunks. The upper quarter has the dense green needle foliage. With these trees, it is possible to see a long way through the trunks of the pines. This was especially true as the sun was lowering in the west. You could see the light filtering through the forest. Every so often we rode through an area of logging.

There would be many hectacres of fallen trees that let us ride under open sky for a change. The forests are actively harvested for lumber. In this area of the foret you had to be careful of slugs. The big, slimy, shell-less snails were first rather scarce and I avoided running over them over. As we got further south, more and more of the creatures appeared on the trail until avoiding them was like riding a slalom course. I have to say that I was unable to avoid all the slugs that climbed out of the ferns onto the trail.

Heading further south, we again started to see the number and size of the campgrounds increase as we neared a crossing with road D42 at St. Girons Plage. The time was now after 7:00 PM and we felt that we should look for accommodations in the beach town. We turned right toward the ocean. It was only a few hundred yards to the town. It must have been a fairly new development because there wasn't much there. There was a nice turnabout entering the main and only street. This was marked with a large anchor at its entrance. We rode down an empty street that had only one open café and the only hotel across from it, appropriately named Hotel de la Plage. As we rode past it, there was a couple building the interior of a new restaurant across the street and several closed beach shops. Past there was the ocean with its thundering waves rolling in. The beach was very wide and two or three people were walking on it. Off the main street were a few dozen private houses that seemed to be waiting for the summer season to begin. With the wind from the beach, the north sides of the houses were almost covered up to the roofs with sand. We turned around and rode back to Hotel de la Plage on the sand covered main street. On inquiring at the lobby/bar about openings, we found there were plenty. We were offered our choice of the Blue Room, the Orange Room, or the Yellow Room. We chose the tiny Yellow room because we could see the Atlantic from our window. We had reached our lodging for the night. Although we didn't get as far as we planned with all our bicycle problems, we felt fortunate to get this far. That evening, we had dinner in the hotel restaurant since it was the only one open in St. Girons Plage. We decided over a glass of wine that we would change our route and not head east to Dax, the Roman spa town, the next day, but head straight south toward Bayonne. The extension to Dax would take us 25 miles to the east and make for a long day of cycling. Since we had lost a couple of hours that day, we felt it would be better to keep our sights set on making it to Spain.

The restaurant was actually quite a lively spot. It turned out that the town was hosting the Dutch surfing championship that week and the Swiss championship the next week. This area of the Landes has excellent waves for surfing. The young Dutch surfers livened up the restaurant. We learned that they were staying at the campground we passed at the town's entrance. After visiting over a few beers, we headed up to our room, quite worn out from the long day. We fell asleep to the sound of the surf on the plage.

LANDES TO BASQUELAND

The next morning, I woke up to a cool, cloudy day. Before doing anything but dressing, I went for a walk along the beach. It was refreshing to watch the large waves roll in and breathe the fresh ocean air. After a few minutes, I returned up the sand covered road to the hotel. We had decided to eat breakfast before leaving the hotel. On returning to the hotel I saw that the dining room was black and the lobby/bar area was locked. I went up and packed my panniers. We were all ready to leave by about 8:15 AM. There was still no one to be seen. The staff and the surfers must have stayed up late. We decided not to wait but we had no one to pay. Since it looked like no one was going to arrive soon, we pulled a pamphlet off a rack outside the lobby. We put 55 Euros inside it and slid it under the locked door to the lobby. There was a small grocery store open near the hotel and we stopped and bought water and rolls, not knowing when we would find a café along the forested coast. We rode out of the tiny beach town as sand blew across the road, past the large anchor, and turned south along a very quiet road near the campgrounds. We were soon on the piste cyclable of Vielle St. Girons. We spent the morning riding through the familiar terrain of pines and ferns of the Landes. Before the path came to an end, we viewed a thin strand of pines on a ridge before us. The bare trunks let the eastern light stream under the canopy. As we rode past the trees, the piste cyclable de la cote came to an end. We got onto a very quiet road, D328, and rode on the hilly stretch towards the coast. We crossed the Courant d'Huchet, a small river flowing down from the etage or Lake de Leon. The Landes has many rivers called "courants" that flow downhill to the Atlantic. The Courant d'Huchet is popular with tourists. They can float in flat bottom boats called gallupes ten kilometers from the Etage de Leon on the courant through a wildlife area. There they can observe birds and flowers along the banks as they float past.

The road took us into Moliets-et Maa. On a village map at a quiet turnabout, we noted there were bike trails again on our route. We rode into Moliets through quiet residential areas looking for the bike trail as well as a place for our delayed breakfast. We found a sign and followed it to a restaurant but found breakfast was not part of their menu. We retraced our route to the bike paths and were soon rolling along a smooth path parallel to D652. At a crossroad near the town of Vieux-Boucau, we saw another sign for a restaurant adjacent to one of the hundreds of campgrounds. I didn't think it was going to have breakfast there, either, especially since it was near 11:00 AM, We went in to find out anyhow. The place was the recreation room for the campers. It had big screen TV's on the walls and video games in each corner. The cook came over and we asked if they had breakfast. He asked if we wanted an English breakfast with eggs, potatoes and bacon and we told him that was exactly what we wanted. In a few minutes, he brought out the breakfast with coffee — it was delightful (even if we had to watch the music videos being played on the wall in front of us).

Well nourished, we were anxious to get back on the trail south. We crossed the Courant d'Vieux-Boucau and then paralleled Highway D79. This was a nice trail separated from the road by a few yards. It was densely wooded which kept the path well shaded. However, the bike path ended a few miles further and we were back riding on the side of D79. It was not too busy and we stayed on it until we turned off to Hossegor. Hossegor is a coastal resort town on a large lake. Elegant villas surround the lake. There are ample jogging trails excellent for our bikes along side the lake.

It was here we started seeing the characteristic Basque architecture — houses of half timbers with sloped roofs and red and green shutters. We were now crossing from the Landes region into Basqueland. Basqueland is seven provinces straddling the French/Spanish border.

Three are in France and four in Spain. The Basques are an indigenous people that are thought to have inhabited this area for at least 40,000 years. Their language is unrelated to any other known language and they fought many centuries to keep it alive. We would soon see road signs written in both French and Basque. As we went further south, the image of the Basques in their characteristic berets would soon become more common.

It was only a few more miles for us to ride from D79 to the lake. It was nice riding alongside the lake and we were soon in the town center with rather chic stores and restaurants. We made a stop at a grocery store/bakery to get supplies for lunch. We were hoping for a good spot along the ocean to eat. At the south end of the lake, we crossed the canal bridge into Capbreton, another coastal resort and well known yachting center. We rode toward the sea. We were also looking for the cycle trail that went south from Capbreton. Before we got to the ocean to eat, we found a directional sign for the trail. We turned off the city street into a residential area and followed the directions to the trail. We were soon on another piste cyclable along the small Boudigau River. We passed many cyclists along the trail and eventually found a little clearing along the brushy riverbank and stopped to eat there. We opened our raincoats to sit on and dangled our legs over the bank. We lunched on baguettes and cheese and watched the river drift by. After a rest, we resumed our ride along the trail.

On getting to Labenne-Ocean the trail was supposed to end, according to my Michelin map, but we found that it continued further south. This was nice because we could still ride on a quiet trail before we had to face the inevitably busy roads into Bayonne. We rode a few kilometers on the Ondres-Plage trail. In Ondres-Plage, we rode over to see the Atlantic since it was so close. We hoped to find that the trail continued further south but had no such luck this time. Now we had to ride east on D26 until we hit the busy N10 highway into Bayonne. N10 is a four lane highway with shopping malls, car dealers and large stores on both sides. There was lots of traffic and lots of stoplights. We rode for 15 km through Ondres and Tarnos and crossed a large railroad bridge as we entered Bayonne proper. We knew N10 would get us to the town center but wondered if there was a better route. We saw a man bicycling toward us. He was also loaded with panniers and a map holder. We waved him down to ask if he knew a better way into Bayonne. It turns out he was a German and spoke English. He was returning from a pilgrimage to Santiago de Compostela, 500 miles away in Spain. He was able to direct us to a road that went downhill to the Bayonne train station. From there, we literally coasted down Rue Maubec to cross the Ardour River on the Pont St. Esprit. We were in Grand Bayonne.

Bayonne is the cultural capital of the northern Basque region. It prospered first as an English city in maritime trade. It was finally taken by the French in 1415. Sitting at the confluence of the Ardour and the smaller Nive Rivers, it retains many old timber-framed buildings with the traditional red and green shutters. These mansions are easily seen along the Nive embankment in the Petit Bayonne district. We found directions to the tourist office and a bike path along the Ardour River took us the half mile from the bridge. Inside we were given a list of hotels mostly by the train station. However, the clerk said we could try Hotel Arceaux on this side of the river.

We rode back a few streets and found the hotel on the pedestrian rue de Port Neuf. Surrounding the entrance were confectionaries with displays of famous Bayonne chocolates and boulangeries with pastries stacked in their windows, including the traditional gateau Basque or Basque cake with its black cherry filling. We went into the Hotel Arceaux and climbed to the office on the first level. The office was a living room overrun with antiques and stuffed animals. The clerk told us there were rooms available. We were taken to a drab room in the hotel interior. The only window opened to a stairwell. Karen vehemently said, "This will not do. Is there anything else?" The clerk said there was another room but it was 10 euros more. No problem. He led us up another flight of stairs to the front of the hotel. Entering we were immersed in color. The colors were all purplish. There was a gossamer canopy over the bed in a fuchsia tone. The dressers were bright purple. Large windows opened onto the rue de Port Neuf and it seemed like we could touch the buildings across the street. We even had a view of the Ardour River. We told him that this would be great and settled down on the purple chaise lounge.

Along the Adour River in Bayonne

After a nice rest and shower, we headed down the stairs past our bikes chained to the banister on the ground floor. The Hotel Arceaux is on the narrow street, rue de Port Neuf, which was once a canal and was filled in during an expansion of the city hundreds of years ago. It is now home to chic clothing stores, designer handbag shops and omnipresent shoe stores. We passed our first store selling Basque goods. Very prominent were its red and green berets, Basque linens and towels with its characteristic seven-striped pattern, and locally made espadrilles. Further up the street is the Cathedral St. Marie. It is built in a gothic style which is unusual for this area of France. Its twin spires are among Bayonne's most recognizable landmarks. We jumped on the free shuttle and rode along the ramparts of the old citadel to the small, but pretty, public botanical gardens. We decided to eat at Eau Bistrot on rue Thiers because the menu on their marquee was in English. It was my chance to order the famous Bayonne ham for dinner. We also had gateau Basque for dessert. As we walked back to our hotel on the quiet streets most of the shops were closed. We ascended to our purple retreat and slept with the shuttered windows wide open over rue de Port Neuf.

BAYONNE TO ST. JEAN DE LUZ

The next morning we decided to skip breakfast at the Hotel Arceaux, particularly since it was served in a musty, antique-laden lobby. Instead we elected to eat at the Boulangerie Mauriac directly across the street from our hotel. We ordered coffee and sat at an outdoor table at the edge of the cobblestone street. It was difficult to decide which pastry to choose as we studied the elegantly displayed creations in the shop window. I had a piece of the gateau aux noix, a cake with nuts in a round tin. Karen had a pastis, a brioche style dough with almonds. When our salesgirl brought our pastries to us she also brought pieces of broken Bayonne chocolate to sample with our breakfast. Chocolate in the morning– a good way to start our day!

We packed up our bikes right next to our table and rode down the Rue de Port Neuf toward the Ardour River. We got on the bike trail at the Place de la Liberte and headed west. A few blocks down we stopped to look at the fresh catch in a fish market on the river-bank. We followed the path until the river made a 90° turn to the north. We didn't want to go out of our way west, so we turned off the trail and rode through the city on very congested urban streets. It was only a short time until we rode under a viaduct and left Bayonne and entered the town of Anglet. In a few blocks, we saw a sign for the town's information center and headed uphill toward it. We asked for directions to Biarritz and found we had just a short ride along the interest-ingly named Avenue de la Chambre de Amour. A left turn at the appropriately named Boulevard de la Mer and we were rolling downhill toward the Atlantic. We soon could see La Pointe St. Martin lighthouse on a spot marking the north end of the Biarritz beach, the famous Grande Plage.

Biarritz came into prominence in the mid 19th century when Empress Eugenie persuaded her hus-band, Napolean III, to build a palace for her. The warm waters and nearby mountains made it a perfect vacation spot. With the completion of a railroad line from Paris in 1855, Biarritz became the playground for European society for the next 70 years. Its visitors ranged from Queen Victoria and King Edward VII to Charlie Chaplin and Coco Chanel. We rode out onto the point and sat beneath the lighthouse which had a magnificent view of the coastline of Biarritz. It was too early in the day to climb the lighthouse but it was refreshing to sit back on one of the many benches and breathe in the sea air.

After walking around on the headland, we rode back to the mainland and rode south on Avenue de la l'Imperatrice past elegant Belle Epoque mansions lining the street. We then rode down to the beach and rode along the walkway past the casino, an Art Deco building dating from 1924. At the end of the walkway, we rode past the neo-Gothic church of St. Eugenie. There were a few brave people venturing into the sea in the cool air. We rode up from the beach and onto a series of rocky promontories. There were good views back to the beach and the old fishing harbor. One particular rock, Rocher de la Vierge, is connected to the mainland by an iron walkway built by Alexandre Eiffel of the tower fame. We walked our bikes out to the rocks and watched the waves crash below us.

We went back into Biarritz and rode south past its chic stores in search of lunch. We found a "not so chic" grocery store and got our supplies of baguettes and cheese for a picnic later on. We were soon heading south along the rue de Madrid. We tried to stay next to the ocean but it wasn't always possible. We headed down the busy N10 highway. At Ilbiarritz, we did get a good view of the Atlantic overlooking the Ilbiarritz Golf Club. In the next town, Bidart, we rode down to its public beach and found a nice bench to eat lunch. We had a view over the wide sandy beach with modern condominiums on either side.

On leaving Bidart, we were obliged to go back to N10 and go a few kilometers south to Guéthary. I felt we could go back to the sea and ride into St. Jean de Luz along the ocean from Guéthary. The street to the sea was steep and we glided down past the new art galleries and ice cream parlors. We crossed the train tracks near its station, which had a beautiful ocean view and an adjoining art gallery. However, we didn't find a road heading south.

We cruised past beach houses until the road ended at the plage de Senix. We could see a road on the south side of the beach a few hundred meters away. Now we either had to ride back uphill to N10 or walk across the beach with our bikes. Not being ones to retreat, we carried our bikes down the stairs and plodded across the beach. Our tires were soon covered with sand. I hoped our chains wouldn't get saturated also. The bikes seemed to get harder to push with each step but in the end we reached the road on the south edge of the plage and rode up the slight incline to a road. Soon the sand dried and fell off our tires. We rode through several campgrounds and crossed the train tracks following the only road we saw. We were back on N10 but it was only a short time until we arrived in St. Jean de Luz. The road soon became a busy urban street. We passed city sports parks with fronton courts that exist in every town in Basqueland. These high walls are for playing the traditional Basque game of pelota, the precursor of jai-alai.

Passing shops and cafes, we crossed the Boulevard Thiers and found rue Sopite, on which our final hotel was located. Rue Sopite was a narrow, one-way street with whitewashed buildings with Basque colored red and green shutters on many windows. We rode up to the Hotel Marisa and left our bikes in the driveway to the garage. Mid afternoon was a good time to arrive. Inside we met our host, the delightful Jacques Buffières. Jacques worked his whole life in the hotel industry all over the world. After retiring, he got an opportunity to purchase the Hotel Marisa in his hometown. On inquiring if our suitcase did arrive in the mail, at first he first didn't remember but it did come and was waiting for us in our room. Jacques showed me the garage where we could keep our bicycles and how to access it with the garage door opener. It was only a one-car garage for his personal use. There was a terraced breakfast area overgrown with trees and vines on a surrounding stone wall. We went up to our room, which was well appointed, and opened the Basque shutters for a view of the Atlantic Ocean through the buildings across the street. We then collapsed on the comfortable beds!

After a short rest we ventured into St. Jean de Luz. I thought it was a good idea to check on the train schedule to get our bikes back to Bordeaux. Coming out of the hotel, a left on rue Sopite for less than a block got us to the beach. We followed the walkway separating the grande plage from the restaurants overlooking it. We followed the walkway for a few streets and turned into the narrow pedestrian streets of the old quarter.

Rue Tourasse was filled with restaurants. The outdoor tables were crowded with late afternoon diners enjoying the fresh fish recently brought into the port. On rue Gambetta, we found the most famous church in St. Jean de Luz, Eglise St. Jean Baptiste. It was the site of the wedding of Louis XIV and the Spanish infanta Maria Teresa in 1660. This union cemented the treaty of the Pyrennes and ended the conflicts between Spain and France. Interestingly, in connection with St. Jean de Luz's maritime history, the church nave was built in the form of a ship's hull and overhead dangles a model of a 17th century ship. We passed many shoe stores with the omnipresent display of handmade espadrilles and shops featuring Basque handicrafts.

As we emerged from the old quarter, we could see the train station across the place des Corsaires. We queued up at the ticket window. I explained that I needed to go to Bordeaux on Saturday, two days hence, and needed to take our bikes on board. I was told there was no train that takes bikes on Saturday morning, only at 7:00 PM. I inquired about Friday and the only time was a 7:00 AM train. It turns out that bikes can only be brought on TER trains, Aquitaine regional trains. When I investigated before we left the US, I found there were lots of times to travel but I didn't find out that bicycles were not allowed on certain trains. We didn't have much choice. We had to leave on Friday, cutting short our stay in St. Jean de Luz, or get back to Paris two days late. We knew our time was short since we had to make Spain the next day.

On our way back we stopped at maison de Paries, a traditional Basque confectionary and sampled the local sweets. We got an assortment of marzipan slices, known to the Basque as tourons to eat on our way back to Hotel Marisa. They packed the slices of the almond flavored sweets in a small box and wrapped it with a ribbon. As we walked along the promenade overlooking the beach, we felt guilty about opening the lovingly wrapped box. But we did anyway. We sat on the beach at the end of rue Sopite and finished the tourons before heading into the hotel.

SPAIN AT LAST!

We awoke for the final day of our journey to a light rain. As we looked toward the ocean, a fine mist covered the street below us. We went down to the breakfast room in the Hotel Marisa. It was too wet to sit out on the patio so we sat inside in the breakfast room decorated with paintings of Basque life. We ate leisurely since we didn't have far to travel – only about 12 miles to the Spanish border. It was unusual to prepare to ride without having to pack our panniers on the bikes but today would be a round-trip endeavor.

We rolled out of the garage around 10:00 AM onto rue Sopite, then a few hundred feet along the beach and then rode through the pedestrian streets that were starting to get busy. Just before the train station, we crossed the bridge Pont Charles de Gaulle over la Nivelle River that separates St. Jean de Luz from Ciboure. From the bridge are great views of the harbor filled with colorful pleasure yachts as well as boats unloading their wares on the docks. Across the harbor stands the Maison de L'infante, the colonnaded mansion where the future queen of France lived before her wedding in 1660. On the Ciboure side of the river, we rode past the working docks to the west towards the ocean on Quai Maurice Ravel. Maurice Ravel, the 20th century composer, was born in Ciboure in 1875 at #27 in a 17th century mansion facing the harbor. Unfortunately, the building was covered with scaffolding as it was being renovated so it was impossible to visit.

We continued along the south side of the harbor and as we approached the Atlantic. We could see Fort de Socoa, built in the 17th century to defend the whaling ships within the bay. From here we headed uphill along the ocean on Highway D912. Looking back, we got a beautiful view of St. Jean de Luz although it was still covered in mist. Heading south we were on a fairly quiet, hilly two lane road. To our right was the rugged coastline. We could look down to the ocean from hundreds of feet above the coast. There we had beautiful views of the waves rolling in. We stopped and walked along the top of a seaside cliff and got a view of a layer of fog floating over the jagged rocks at the water's edge. Back on the road there were several moderate climbs and quick descents as we followed the unspoiled shoreline. After about 10 miles, we glided down a long, curved hill and entered the flat beachfront of Hendaye, the last town in France before the Spanish border. Within minutes, we left the undeveloped coastline and were now on a bike path bordering a long, flat sandy beach with ice cream parlors, small hotels and restaurants across the road. Hendaye is a popular resort city and is known for its fine surfing. As we rode along the Grande Plage, we saw dozens of surfers. There were also surfing schools with children receiving instruction while on their boards in the water.

We followed the straight road along the beach and assumed we would get to the border at the end of the beach. As parking lots started filling up, we rode the few miles to the Bidassoa River, the dividing line between France and Spain. We could see the town of Fuenterrabia with its cathedral on the hills across the river. However, we found no bridge to cross. We turned inland to follow the river and soon got trapped in a large harbor of pleasure boats and no way to cross the river. We had to retrace our route and head away from the river a mile or so until we could ride around the harbor. We then followed a biking/jogging path uphill with a good view of the harbor until we found a street heading south towards the train station. This was an area of narrow streets with run-down shops and buildings around the station. We rode through an industrial area by the rail yards and soon saw a bridge over the Bidassoa. It was an old unimpressive metal bridge. There was no sign signifying the border with Spain. The only designation was a sign that said "Irun", the Spanish city across the Bidossoa River. There were two men fishing off the bridge and we asked them to take our picture documenting the end of our odyssey. I always thought that picture would contain some sort of marker proving we were crossing into Spain. But our photograph shows Karen and I standing with our bikes on a rusty old bridge!

The little bridge to Spain

We then headed towards Fuenterabia. It was very industrial and we turned up a ramp on a small, limited access road with oil tanks across from us and a small airport to our right. We decided this was as far into Spain as we would travel. One thing about our bike tours is that we never had to turn around. Since we were staying in St. Jean de Luz and had to go back, the realization that we would have to retrace our route made our decision to not go further into Spain an easy one.

We rode back to the river on the busy roads. At the border, we stopped at a bodega and bought a bottle of

Spanish wine. From there we found another bridge. This one was not used for vehicles. There was a class of students from Bordeaux studying the ecology of the bay area. The teachers said they often come to this area for field trips. We told them about our travels from Bordeaux. They tried to help us with our train dilemma and offered to bring our bikes back with them on the school bus. I considered their offer briefly. The ride back to St. Jean de Luz went quickly. We had a lunch at a sandwich shop on the Hendaye beach and rode the hilly seaside roads back. Things always seem shorter on a return trip!

In St. Jean de Luz, we stopped on the promenade along the beach and drank the Spanish wine, realizing that we had succeeded in our dream to bicycle across France from Belgium to Spain. That evening, we celebrated by having a traditional dinner at Restaurant le Portua along the walking street Rue de la Republic. We sat at a nice outdoor table covered with a blue and white checked tablecloth and watched people amble along the narrow street. Le Portua specializes in traditional seafood of the coast. We got a bottle of the local wine, a red, fruity, Irouleguy wine from the area south of Bayonne. We ordered paella maison, which was seafood paella. This was served in an enormous wrought iron skillet filled with creatures from the nearby ocean. The oysters and clams were tasty, the langostinos (small, lobster-like crustaceans) were served whole. I have always been uncomfortable eating things with eyes that looked back at me but we managed to finish most of the meal. For dessert, we had profiteroles, an éclair-like pastry filled with cream and covered in an almond syrup. An espresso capped the meal.

On returning to the hotel, I asked Jacques if we could have a wake-up call. We needed to be up just past 5:00 AM the next morning to catch our train. He told me there was an automated system on our telephone. I tried to set it up from our room but the instructions were all in French — there was no way I was going to get it to work. I called the front desk, "Jacques, you must come up and set up the alarm for me." A few minutes later, he was upstairs and with the pressing of a few buttons it was set. I just hoped it would work. That night we opened the shutters on the windows and laid back in bed. The smell of the ocean drifted into our room as we fell asleep.

LEAVING ST. JEAN DE LUZ

At 5:00 AM we were jolted out of our sleep when the phone rang just as Jacques programmed it to do. It was pitch dark outside and a light drizzle was falling. We quickly dressed and packed our panniers and suitcase. I wasn't sure if we could get our bikes and suitcase to the station in one trip. Then the phone rang again. There was a female voice on the line and I am not sure what she said or who it was. I believe Jacques asked his wife to call to make sure the wake-up call worked. A human check of technology! We got our bags to the elevator and went down to the lobby. We got the garage door opener from behind the desk and opened the garage door. You didn't need to go outside to open it. We went out and removed our bikes from the narrow garage. We didn't have much trouble transporting our gear. We strapped our one suitcase on the back of one of the bikes and put all the panniers on the other and walked to the train station. We left the hotel walking down Rue Sopite to the sea wall and got our last look at the Atlantic as the dawn was breaking. We walked our bikes up Rue Garat, past the shuttered stores, into the station in plenty of time for our train to Bordeaux.

We waited on the platform as dawn turned into day. When the train arrived the conductor showed us to the car with the bike racks. There were actually hooks on the wall like you'd have in your garage to hang the bikes vertically. We found a seat and settled down for the short trip to Bordeaux. We passed the quaint station in Guethary with its art gallery and café. We might even have dosed off. We got to Bordeaux and let the train empty before attempting to disembark. We had two bikes, as well as a suitcase, to negotiate but we managed to get everything to the platform. We had to find a luggage locker to store our gear. We reloaded the bikes as we did in St. Jean de Luz and walked into the station, then down a ramp to a lower level to cross under the tracks. There were tunnels to the street but we found we had to get one level up to get to the baggage check area. We didn't find an elevator and the escalators were not a good idea in our situation. We got to the main area of the station with its massive stone staircase. We decided it was easiest to just unload the bikes and carry them up the stairs. It took a few trips and I suppose we were an unusual sight carrying our bikes up the staircase in the center of the station. We reloaded the bikes, went onto the platform and walked to the side where the baggage check was located. We brought our gear inside the caged area, went through the x-rays, got change from the machine and locked our gear away. Now we had 2½ hours to return our bikes and catch our train out of Bordeaux.

It was nice to get on our bikes unencumbered by packs. We knew that Station Velo Services was not too far from the Gare St. Jean. We rode away from the station down the busy urban street Cours de la Marne staying in the designated bus lane on the right. It made for a nice ride unless a bus came up behind us. It seemed like a longer ride on the shop-lined street than I thought it would be but soon we recognized the Marche des Capuchins, the outdoor market set amongst the ugly, modern, academic buildings of the University. We turned left for our final two block stretch down Cours de l'Yser and rolled into the Station Velo Services bike shop. Fortunately, it was open and both Emmanuel and Victor were there. "We're back," I announced. They asked about our adventures of the last week and, surprisingly, knew all about our defective wheel dilemma. More surprisingly, they cordially apologized for the trouble we had with the bike and refunded us for the cost to replace the wheel in Mimizan-le-Plage. I can't express what a nice feeling it gave me to deal with the considerate, French people. We shook hands, said adieu, patted the bikes good-bye and walked into the busy streets of Bordeaux.

Made in the USA
Columbia, SC
28 March 2021